The Hillside Diary and Other Writings

The Hillside Diary and Other Writings

by Robert Gary Neugeboren

Edited and with an introduction by Jay Neugeboren

CENTER *for* PSYCHIATRIC REHABILITATION
Sargent College of Health and Rehabilitation Sciences
Boston University

Published by:

Center for Psychiatric Rehabilitation
Sargent College of Health and Rehabilitation Sciences
Boston University
940 Commonwealth Avenue West
Boston, MA 02215
http://www.bu.edu/cpr/

The Center for Psychiatric Rehabilitation is partially funded by the National Institute on Disability and Rehabilitation Research and the Center for Mental Health Services, Substance Abuse and Mental Health Services Administration.

Printed in the United States of America

Cover and book design by Linda Getgen

Library of Congress Control Number: 2003111601

ISBN 1-878512-15-3

ROBERT NEUGEBOREN was born in Brooklyn, New York, in 1943. He attended public schools there, won a New York Regents State Scholarship and attended City College of New York. In his early years, he had leads in many dramatic productions, and starred in several musicals. He has spent a large portion of his adult years in mental hospitals, supervised residences, and halfway houses, and for the last several years has been living in the Clinton Residence in the Hell's Kitchen section of New York City. He is a member of New York City's Fountain House, where he works in various capacities, and is featured in the documentary film *Imagining Robert*.

JAY NEUGEBOREN is the author of fourteen books, including two prize-winning novels, *The Stolen Jew* and *Before My Life Began*, and two award-winning books of nonfiction, *Imagining Robert* and *Transforming Madness*. His most recent book is *Open Heart: A Patient's Story of Life-Saving Medicine and Life-Giving Friendship*. He is featured in the documentary film *Imagining Robert*. Professor and Writer-in-Residence at the University of Massachusetts for thirty years, he now lives in New York City.

contents

Introduction

I have told the story before.

"In October 1973," I wrote in *Imagining Robert*, "when our parents retired and moved to Florida, they shipped about twenty cartons of Robert's belongings to me in Massachusetts—books mostly, but also clothing, records, framed prints and drawings, his stamp collection, his 16mm Bell and Howell Model 70 movie camera, his chess set (a gift from me for his Bar Mitzvah), and personal items Robert referred to as his 'rememorabilia.' They asked me to store them for him against the day when, they hoped, he would be well again and would have a life and home of his own."

First hospitalized in 1962, and hospitalized more than fifty times since then, my brother Robert has spent most of his adult life—forty years—in mental hospitals and psychiatric wards in and around New York City. The list is long: Hillside, Creedmoor, South Beach, Bronx Psychiatric Center, Mid-Hudson Psychiatric Center, Gracie Square, Bellevue, Kings County, and others. He has also been homeless, and has lived in various apartments, group homes, SROs, and supervised residences.

In 1997, when he was living on a locked ward at the South Beach Psychiatric Center, his therapist, angry at the way he had been (pseudonymously) portrayed in *Imagining Robert,* stated— after harrassing me with, among other threats, the possibility that the staff would have to use electroshock on Robert (the treatment Robert feared above all, as the therapist knew)—that on a scale of one to ten, the possibility of Robert living outside a locked ward was one.

After *Imagining Robert* appeared in 1997, however, Robert and I received hundreds of letters and calls, including some from mental health professionals like Dr. Alvin Pam, Director of Psychology at Bronx State, who offered to help. Dr. Pam suggested a transfer to his hospital. "No promises," he said, "but if Robert is willing to give us a chance here at Bronx State, we'd like to work with him. We think we can do better."

Robert agreed to the transfer. When he first arrived at Bronx State, however, it was the consensus of the staff, Dr. Pam later told me, that Robert might never be able to live outside the locked ward of a state hospital. Dr. Pam disagreed. Two years later Robert was discharged from Bronx State and began living at the Clinton Residence, a group home administered by Project Renewal, and located on West 48th Street in the Hell's Kitchen section of New York City. The residence, a handsome, seven-story red brick building adjacent to one of the city's more beautiful neighborhood-run gardens, is home for fifty to sixty men and women, all of whom, like Robert, have experienced long-term serious and persistent mental illness.

For someone diagnosed as mad, he is, in matters of human connection and affection, remarkably realistic and sane.

Nearly four years later (I am writing this in the late summer of 2003) Robert is still living at the Clinton Residence—the longest stretch in his adult life that he has not been hospitalized. He has friends, he goes to museums and restaurants, he shops in the neighborhood, he visits with me and other members of our family, he makes trips out of the city, and he gets around the city on his own by subway, bus, and taxi. He takes classes—horticulture, poetry, photography—and he also works, for pay, one day a week.

When people inquire about his life now—he is sixty years old—he often says that he is "semi-retired." But how do you spend most of your days, a cousin asked at a recent Passover Seder. "How do I spend my days?" he replied, and gave what seemed to him the obvious answer: "I smoke and I drink coffee." Then, seeing the surprise on our cousin's face, he laughed.

Among the items our parents sent north to me in 1976 was a cherry wood trunk that had belonged to one of our neighbors, and that had been given to us after the neighbor's death. When, in the spring of 1991, I began work on *Imagining Robert*, I opened the trunk, and found, among other items—overdue library books, Robert's tefillin, drawings, photos, underwear, ashtrays Robert had made at Hillside (because they were "cracked," Robert called them "psycho-ceramics")—a thick pale-green binder which, I assumed, contained Robert's poems.

When I opened the binder, however, what I found was a typed manuscript of some one hundred pages and on the title page, this:

From the diary of a nineteen year old
mental patient named
robert gary neugeboren
p.o. box 38
glen oaks, n.y.

Robert kept his diary, which he shared with his therapists, for about six weeks, from April 3 to May 15, 1962. "Each time I go through Robert's diary," I wrote in *Imagining Robert*, "I find myself wanting to read it aloud to everyone I know—and to publish it entire, not only because it gives such a vivid, moving, and often delightful account of his daily life at Hillside, and of the way this kind of private institution cared for the mentally ill thirty years ago, but—more important—because it gives a sense of Robert in Robert's own words: of who he was at nineteen, and of what a full and idiosyncratic life, imagination, mind, and identity he had."

That wish, made a dozen years ago, has now come true.

While working on *Imagining Robert*, I also read through dozens of Robert's poems, and hundreds of letters he had sent to me and to our parents. I included excerpts from all three—the diary, poems, and letters—in the book. When, in 1997, Florentine Films/Hott Productions began filming a documentary based on *Imagining Robert*, Larry Hott, the producer, had Robert recite some of his poems, and also asked him to read, on camera, from his diary and letters.

And when I approached the Boston University Center for Psychiatric Rehabilitation about the possibility of publishing Robert's diary entire, I suggested that they include with it a selection of Robert's poems and letters. Happily, they agreed, and so, along with the complete text of *The Hillside Diary*, we have here included several dozen of Robert's poems, and a generous selection of his letters.

The letters begin in 1958, when Robert was a junior at Erasmus Hall High School in Brooklyn and I was a senior at Columbia, and they end in 1976, the year of our father's death. Given that the letters provide, in themselves, a narrative of Robert's life during these years and, thus, a vivid and fascinating context for the diary, some readers may prefer to read the letters first, or to move back and forth between the diary and the letters.

Along with the poems and the diary, the letters provide a rich, textured portrait of an extraordinary young man and of the struggles he was going through during his early years. They also give us a detailed, often poignant sense of what life was like for people who were mental patients back then—and of how the daily and ongoing experience of being a mental patient, and being treated as one, both in and out of institutions, public and private, made itself felt in their lives.

Although I have read Robert's writings often through the years, what impressed me all over again when I read them this time was Robert's extreme generosity of spirit, and his optimism. No matter the struggles, defeats, sadness, absurdity, or pain that inform his life, Robert rarely loses his desire to care for and about others, or his sheer love of this world.

"Wee! what a wonderful day," he exclaims at the start of a diary entry early on during his first long-term (eighteen month) hospitalization. "Just took a shower painted another picture and am listening to some good music—all is right with the world." Two weeks later, this: "listening to henry miller on the phonograph and hearing another man say that man is lonely, I recognized the shadow of myself seeking and reeking from aloneness. And every so often i remember that call it what ever you may but I am in a mad house. Cheerful, no?"

When he is given a pass out of the hospital, he describes his time away in joyful understatement. "Was walking around the outside like a free man in his right mind," he writes. Several years later, however, when he is hospitalized yet again, this time in an institution for the criminally insane, though his humor is still alive, his joy is muted with bitterness. "If you show your faces or feces at the weddings," he writes to me, "...and they ask after me (you know Jay didn't you once have a brother and there was something wrong with him there was even a book about him painting his pictures out of an institution) tell them I smoke cigars and really do love them and that with my next face lift I'll look better than never."

Robert's writings are filled with descriptions of his daily doings—what he ate, who he ate with, what he is reading, what movies he saw, etc.—and they are also filled with descriptions of what is most precious to him: his friends, and his relationships with his friends. The listings may sometimes seem perfunctory (he believes his therapist wants him to record his days in a particular way and order), yet the quotidian often opens to moments of wonder and grace, and Robert renders these moments for us in idiosyncratic prose that transforms the ordinary into the extraordinary.

"Came back to the low and forgot to get a sandwich for bob—met him and played some ping pong and then asked if he wanted to go visit cindy—he did and we went," one passage begins. Then: "We all went into the back yard and started kicking around a dead volleyball, then we got to playing ping pong with a volleyball and i beat cindy. Then we just lay on the grass and talked silly nothings and then it got darker. We went inside and got attacked by some old ladies."

When he is given a pass out of the hospital, he describes his time away in joyful understatement. "Was walking around the outside like a free man in his right mind," he writes.

Robert's humor—sometimes broad, often understated, invariably ironic—is ever-present. When a team of doctors ask him about how and why he became ill—about his first psychotic break—he answers directly; a few moments later, he notes his reaction to what one of the doctors tells him. "Told me i had a rather traumatic life which was encouraging because i thought i was just overdramatizing."

His film and literary criticisms are shrewd and original—"*The Court Martial of Billy Mitchell*," he writes in his diary, "could have been a radio broadcast for all the camera added to it." When he writes to me from a mental hospital about *The Greening of America*, he is unequivocal and clear-eyed. "What a turkey!" he writes. "This guy Charles A. Reich quotes Marcuse Marx and some others but the whole affaire is like a Reader's Digest reworking of a Sunday times special supplement on don't worry folks your children are justified in wearing long hair."

Most of all, though, Robert's writings are filled with small dramas that have large issue. His affection for and devotion to his friends is unwavering, and his sadness when they become lost—in madness, in drugs, in the world—is matched by his desire to help and to love. For someone diagnosed as mad, he is, in matters of human connection and affection, remarkably realistic and sane. "Then asked [Cindy] what she did today," he writes, "and she said nothing in a very depressed way and i tried to cheer her up by telling her that a watched pot never boils and that she had to start somewhere even if it were anywhere and that after a while she would begin to get involved in things but that she mustn't watch herself so closely. She said that she enjoyed nothing and i tried to disprove her—then i asked her if she would like to come to the library and she said she didn't care, but that she never spoke with anyone like she did with me, and thanked me then. She signed out and came. I showed her the Steinberg book and she laughed but then her aid came and she told the aid that she signed out but we both giggled because she is on restrictions. The aid came back and so cindy finally—third time—she got an aid to stay with her. In between i wrote this poem:

the love between us
grows like ivy
poisoned and itchy
it goes up and down my skin-shell
goosing me into pimples
and all i know
blows away before your asking heart."

Robert also seems remarkably sane about his own situation and condition—and as open and honest with others (our parents, his friends, his doctors) as he is with himself. "First called mother," he writes on the first day of Passover, "to wish her a happy pesach and she decided to give me a lecture. Said the doctors said i was very sick and that I had too many friends on the week end i told her to stop it and we both hung up." Then this: "I know i'm sick probably better than anyone it is me who feels un free and depressed and inferior and slightly paranoid nobody else, it is me who finds it hard to sit still and concentrate. it is I who haven't been able to communicate with people what the hell is she complaining about. I am perfectly honest with the doctors and my parents what do they want it takes time and more time. It took how many millions of years to produce me and my environment I can't get well overnight."

In *Imagining Robert,* with Robert's help, I tried to place the story of our relationship as brothers, and of Robert's life as a mental patient, within the context of a family history. Now, in his diary, poems, and letters—in his own words, and in a book of his own— Robert tells his story.

A Note on the Text

Robert's spelling is often idiosyncratic: "hungry" is "hungary," "relationships" is "realationships," "William Saroyan" is "William Sayroyan," "boring" is "booring," "raisin bran" is "raison-bran," and he often makes up words: "tensious" (a combination of tension and anxious), "headance" (for headache), "effeminency," "autotorium," "beef stronganoff," etc. He rarely capitalizes names or other nouns (including, most of the time, the "i" ["I"] of his narrative), and punctuation, like spelling, is inconsistent and erratic.

I have retained virtually all original spellings and punctuation, but here and there have broken lengthy sections into separate paragraphs, and I have made minor corrections when misspellings are mere typographical errors. In order to protect the privacy of people mentioned in the diary and letters, I have, in many instances, used pseudonyms. Otherwise, what you are about to read, beginning with "The Hillside Diary," came forth once upon a time from the mind, heart, and imagination of a young man named Robert Gary Neugeboren.

Jay Neugeboren
New York City
August 2003

The Hillside Diary

From the diary of a nineteen year old

mental patient named

robert gary neugeboren
p.o. box 38
glen oaks,n.y.

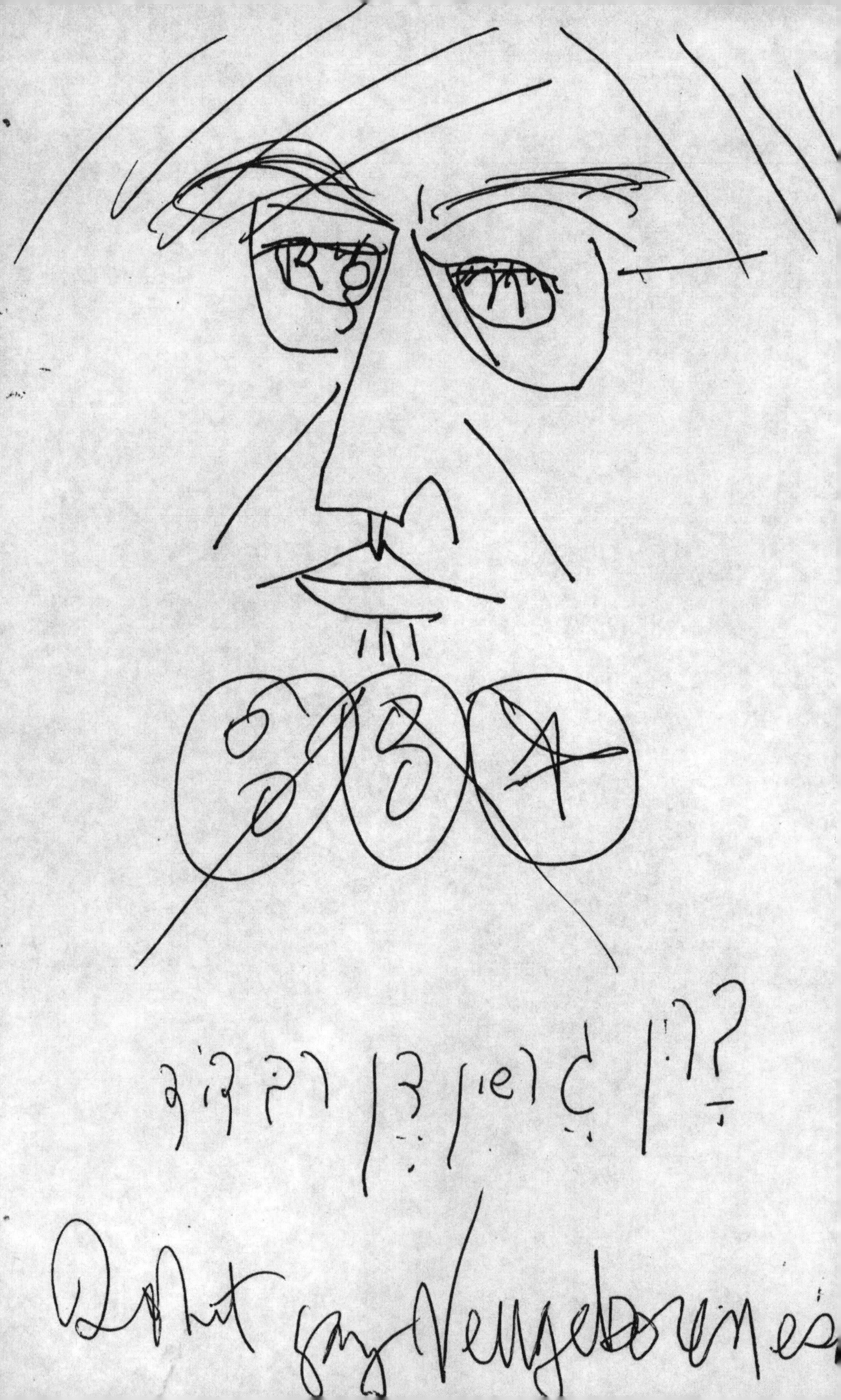
Don't say

3 april, 1962 — (done on Thursday the 12)

I shall go through the day trying to remember what has happened and how i happended this wednesday in april.

I awoke at eight after dreaming of a circus but I don't remember who i was in the circus or what i was doing — associated it with the contest that the activities committee is sponsoring on night activities. I changed my linen (they have a thing called linen exchange where you bring last week's dreamed in and creamed in sheets in exchange for nice soft white new sheets, pillowcases and towels). Then i rushed to breakfast had oatmeal and raison-bran and sugar smacks and three juices and a cup of luke warm coffee. I still haven't learned how to drink hot coffee yet. Talked with Marty (Silver) and Roz, spoke of the sixth grade and how i used to urinate out the window at ps 181. Also told —-tickle-your-ass-with a feather — particularly-nasty-weather, and may-I-fuck-your-daughter — would-you-like-a-glass-of-water. (last night we had bananasplit on cake for dessert and i asked Roz if i might have her (whip) cream, she replied yes "but don't touch my banana," to which the girls at the next table cracked up). I then washed off the acromel (that is some sort of fleshy-coloured ointment that the doctor has prescribed for my acne — I feel guilty knowing that if i but washed, my pimples would go away — tonight for sure i will take a shower.) I was dressed in my dungerees and a tee shirt with out my hair combed. I then went to "Music Appreciation," which was downstairs in the patients lounge. They were playing "Peer Gynt Suite" by Grieg and it was very relaxful. I stretched out on the couch and waited for sleep to overcome me. It did and about a half minute later Mrs. Krochmal (one of the morning nurses) woke me saying 'Robert it is time to go to your work group.' I yelled a little, protesting that i did not want to do the busy work repainting already painted furinture. (Mrs. Stevens, our usual occupational leader, is on a one week vacation.) She said it was good for my therapy and i knew that i should go so I did. Mrs. Ely (?) was waiting and i decided to paint a little cabinet. We (there must be six of us?) cover all the painted "wood" (an ugly stain like the antique stain that momma did to all of the beautiful inlaid furniture that we got [after] Aunt Esther died) with a bright tan. It is boring work but it is supposed to be part of my therapy—it is called "milieu therapy" because of the importance of everything that is done by and for the patient in this hospital. I finished the cabinet and went on to a headboard. Mr. Payne (an aide) brought me a doctors' appointment slip for 11:30 and i was happy that Dr. Plaut was going to see me in the morning. This was my first morning appointment since I've been here.

I think I am happier in the morning because i have faith that a new day has just dawned and there are going to be new things that i can learn and see and be with. I took a coffee break and went to the bathroom. Didn't try to masturbate as i did the morning before. It seems that when i am boored the most i resort to masturbation to ease my almost anxieties. But thorazine keeps away most of my tensious (tension and anxiety) attacks. We did some painting and then started cleaning up.

I left previously and took a walk down to Creative Therapy to see sad Helen. She hadn't painted anything yet but two people, one awful nervous man and a woman, were analzying a sketch she did. I saw one girl's picture—a copy of Roualt's "Biblical Exodus" (I think it was called). It is a beautiful Roualt with a prancing horse and two figures on a landscape, with the golden sun and of course lots of black. Denny Klein, and here i associate Danni from, Winterset, and why hasn't Ulla rewritten me—did i say something wrong in the last letter? And I left together and he made some mention of tennis (I am to teach him tennis in exchange for his teaching me chess, and of course other things—I do not feel inferior to him, just subordinate—he is reputed to have 180 I. Q.) but i answered that i had a D. A. [*Doctor's Appointment*] at 11:30 and anyway it was too cold out.

The weather was sort of damp up till then, with puddles here and there. So i went back to the low and decided that i would get dressed for dear old Esther [*Plaut*] and myself, being at the last session i had said some of my desire to change and become a neat young man. I chose my grey shirt, brown slacks and red tie and tennis sneakers.

I arrived at the waiting room about two minutes early (I am not too anxious about theapy sessions), hoping that i would not have to wait a half hour like i did on Monday. The Dr. opened the door and let Alan (Weinberg) out and said "Mr. Neugeboren," so i put the "Today's Health" down and went into her office, she said hello. Immediately i told her that i should have gotten mad on Monday because of the half hour wait, instead it seemed that she was mad at me. She didn't understand and said that Mrs. Krochmal must have made a misteak but that it was good that i told her so that now she knew, etc. She told me that i would have to stop seeing my friends that they were interfering with my therapy. I got sulky and resentful—the weekend was what i looked forward to and here she was taking my friends away. But she said that i made these friends when i was sick and that therefore they were mixed up and would only mess me up further. I understood what she was saying and she will allow me to see relatives so things are not too bad. I can have a friend if she agrees.

Then she tried to wring out of me why and what happened just before i got hospitalized. I quickly tried to communicate how depressed and apathetic and like a child i was. Some of my fears. She didn't seem to get what she wanted and i guess it takes a while before either of us understand exactly what was going on.

I ate lunch—stuffed turkey, sweet potato and ?—saw Dr. Plaut on line but what was there for the two of us to say? O yes during the session i wanted to know why everyone was so interested in me and said that she must enjoy seeing people get better and then stuck in that I saw Tommy Stewart last night and he was going to school and looked happy and maybe someday i could be like that. She asked me what i wanted and i said to have a girl and be happy to understand the world around me and to love those who love me.

She said they weren't unreasonable demands and that maybe i could achieve most if not all of these goals.

She asked me what i wanted and i said to have a girl and be happy to understand the world around me and to love those who love me.

Ate lunch with a somewhat pretty lady from low 2 and discussed the fact that she was getting out soon—asked her if she felt better and she said somewhat. Played volleyball after lunch and left after two good games. Wandered in the library and tried to read the N. Y. Times but was not interested. Bob (Gold) was there and I asked him to give [me] some art lessons. He did and it was great. He showed me how in a good painting things, masses rest on other masses and that the space of air left around the object was very important. Started reading a pamphlet on Jackson Pollack, wow! I want to action paint—came back to the ward and saw Bob (Miller) in a dopey mood, asked him if he wanted to play ping pong. We did but i was scared that he would pass out but none of the aides seemed concerned about his greenness. We later went to hear some music—Brahms i think—and he read the Pollack book and i talked to Allan Weinberg and somehow managed to tell him of my operation [orchiectomy].

Then i was told to make my bed and i did. I finished reading the Pollack pamphlet and went to dinner with Morris. Dinner was grilled cheese and bacon and ice cream. I had three ice-creams and one of them tasted funny. We were giggling—Marty, Tim James, and Cindy (Abrams), when Cindy started washing her face with two grilled cheese sanwhiches—then she took mustard and slapped it on her face all the while hysterical with laughter. She wiped it off. I asked Tim if he was going to go to current events class and he said no. I left the dining room in a cheerful mood and met the twins—Betty and barbara, with Sam (Ware) and Roz. They were going outside the gate for a walk into town. I decided i would sneak out with them just for the fun.

I saw a beautiful blackbird with white tailfeathers. I also saw a large type bird that they said was a quail or dove it was beautiful. We ran past the gate but i decided that i wanted to get better and disciplined so i said i was going back and i did. Going back i saw a sight. A doctor, youngish, was wearing a beret swimging a briefcase and singing "Hava Negila" just like I would do. So maybe i am not so sick after all.

> Going back i saw a sight. A doctor, youngish, was wearing a beret swimging a briefcase and singing "Hava Negila" just like I would do. So maybe i am not so sick after all.

I went to current events but after five minutes i said to myself what was i doing here with all these nebishes? I should be outside enjoying nature. So I left and took a walk—remembered that Smith was going to open the library. They have nice chairs with armrests in the library, also a nice phonograph. I put on a piano concerto by Beethoven. And i took out a big art book entitled "The Lasker Collection". It was beautiful—Dufys and Matisses and Picassos... then i quickly looked through a book on Gaugin and saw some of his watercolours for the first time. The man is a semi-genius. I came out of the library reeling with colors, maroons and oranges. I would do another painting. A still life with the fruits (not fruit) that i had back in my room. Two oranges a banana and apple. I worked only with a pallette knife, improvising a dark shining blue background—the only definite shape is the banana—maybe I'll outline them in black. Played some ping pong and then to the evening activity which was dancers and a singer.

I came in and walked right to the front row and there tried to look under the dancers' wide skirts but saw nothing. I saw Bob and Helen sitting on the opposite side and planned to stay with them, my friends. What makes a friend why did i pick them to be friendly with? Who knows. Then Sarah, who is in the choral club with me started singing with a magnificent dramatic soprano voice and the evening activity was over.

I came back and tried to do some reading from—space-time and architecture but my eyes became blurry. Listened to Brahms, went to the toilet and started typing this. Talked with William and found it hard falling asleep. Dreamt of a trial or a composition about a trial. woke at 8:15.

Thursday, April 12, 1962

little chips of diamonds
dandruff for my hair
melting in april
*

black on green
do you grow like seeds
and what makes you fly when i come near?
*

green webs on grey, today
tomorrow waving webs with blue
mixed with yellow bolts

I woke a little earlier than usual this morning and went to the bathroom and washed off the acromel. Went to breakfast in my dungarees and yellow sweatshirt. Had raison bran, farina and two grapefruits. Talked with Candy. Can't remember very much else that happened this morning. Went to O. T. and painted three head-boards ran away once to see creative therapy and Helen and Bob (Ware) a surprise—Cindy (Abrams) was painting or rather copying Modigliani's "Gypsy with Child." That girl is so talented, beautiful and winning that i want to love her, but in my pesent condition who knows if i can really love another human being humanly. I know that i am beginning to love or respect myself, being proud of silly little things, but they are still things and I am getting better. So Cindy will have to wait and meanwhile maybe the both of us can become happy, free, and creative.

I called up mother and spoke for less than three minutes it was alright and she wants me so to be happy and well that it is as though i have a responsibility to other people as well as myself.

Had a government meeting after lunch and i cracked a few jokes typical—the ward is having trouble waking up in the morning so we are gong to have a wake up committee of which i am a member, so i said maybe we should have a tucker-in committee, or get some girls to wake me up. Government meetings are funny and nice democratic institutions i see the need for them and how they help patients to be part of a group. I suggested that handles be put in the bathtub but somebody said they were removed because some one tried to hang himself—a rather pleasant thought, no? I played three games of ping pong with Donnie (Rudnick) and lost all of them, but my game is improving and i find it a great release until the weather will get better so that I can play tennis. I saw Dr. Plaut and asked if I could be let home for the sedars—she went into a long speech which rather annoyed me i mean if the

answer is no it is no. But she did have her reasons and i agreed (why did I want to go home in the first place? Am I getting more religious—no but i am beginning to love rituals—they are so self contained and beautiful almost like exercises or fugues.) She notified me that she put me on the list for creative therapy which was nice news, but the wait will probably be long—I really don't know how long i can paint furniture and feel as though my therapy is progressing. The dr. asked that question on Wednesday as to why feelings of responsibility, why must i always feel as though I am doing something important i quickly replied that it was probably a reaction to my father's doing nothing and the fact that i don't want to feel useless or like a nothing that mother always used to say I'd become.

```
Thursday April 12,1962
little c hips of diamonds
d randruff for my hair
melting in april

*

RReeXxxof black on green
do you grow like seeds
and what makes you fly when i come near?

*

green webs on grey,today
tomorrow waving webs with blue
mixed with yellow bolts
```

It was then three o'clock and time for dramatics which I wasn't really looking forward to. Well I went and stayed till fifteen after and then decided that Music Appreciation would be more fun so went to the Patients' Lounge. Miss Lopez was reading from the back of a jacket in broken english about program music and Vivaldi, she played spring and summer. The violins were quite something, but still i was bored so i left took a walk and ended up in the library but the library was closing. I returned to the low wandered around for a while then I got that starey feeling and knew

that I wanted to do some reading writing and painting all at once
also listen to some music. I put on Orff's "Die Kluge" in Tim's
room, and got a canvass and made a design which I thought illus-
trated Bob's lesson from yesterday. It has a low diving line with sort
of cherries on the bottom reversing every other one, the top has
two eliptical shapes repeating themselves three times, they are quite
phallic (I think). It has a red background yellow elliptoids with
black and then a ring of blue. It is quite static and i don't
know how to give it movement.

Then I remembered that I had K. P. and ran to the
dining room. I didn't see anyone else on K. P. so I took
my dinner, ham, cabbage and potatoes with chocolate
cake, I rushed through my meal and then found out that
I have it on another day. By this time Candy sat down
next to me and we exchanged pleasantries—she is quite
a positive girl and i am beginning to like her, except that
she is twenty five and I will be nineteen. We moved into
another room because we seemed to pick the teenage
lounge which was awfully noisy. We moved in to a room
where Larry, Pat and Bob, along with Bob Selig were
having a good time so we joined them. I sang off key—
whoopee and ninety nine bottles of beer on the wall and
friends and other camp favorites we were really quite
wild. I then met a volunteer lady who was to lead the
sketching class—she was wearing a magnificent black
silk coat and was very charming.

I then went to science class which was a boor. It was
about Atomic Energy but the girl who was leading it
was a physics major at Queens with aspirations of
becoming a social worker and she hadn't prepared very much so we
had a discussion much along the lines of what scientists can do—I
frolicked in the hall with Cindy and Bob for two minutes and then
went into the sketching class (I forgot to mention that Mrs. Lewis,
a nurse, brought a copy of Heronious Bosch which was lots of fun,
and she gave me a turkish cigarette that made my nose and tongue
tingle, that was around four) the sketching class is going to do a
mural in the dining room which I want to be part of. Kibbitzed for
awhile and asked the lady for a cigarette—she gave me a magnifi-

cent Pall Mall and then I went back to the low 2 to tell Helen that "someone was waiting outside the newspaper office ready to play with her"—a message that Bob G. had made me promise that I would give to her. Roz saw me, came up and gave me a magnificent kiss and we hugged. I complained that I would have to go to teen lounge and she said that she would sneak in. We waited in the hall and joked for a while mostly about lesbians and masterbation. I took her and Susan into my room to see my paintings—they liked my sea scape and the three latest ones (I shall number then now. And take my thorazine—be back shortly.) no. 8 particularly, and i think it is my sloppiest, it has hardly any forms but it has movement, which people love.

Then I went to the teen lounge, did a twist with Heather, introduced myself to a new girl—Jenny—she looks about sixteen but is twenty-one, not very pretty looking but a "nice quiet girl"—wonder what her problems are—not mature probably, blocking at sixteen who knows?—I'm no dr. yet. Talked with the stupid group leader on how i wanted to go to the adult lounge. Roz came, fat as ever and we decided we'd take a walk around the quadrangle. She let me hold her hand and we talked and walked and then went to the Adult lounge but Maryse (a nurse) was there to tell me get back to the low. I did and read time magazines art collection for about five issues. Watched a half hour Dr. Kildare about alcoholics and thank heavens my body is free and i don't need things. Then I started typing up the day. Hope to read some Jimanez and do some scribbling. end.

Friday April 13, 1962

Another day gone by and now i am depressed again. But I'll start from the morning since that is where i started this day with. Rose early but not early enough to wake anyone else up. Washed and went to breakfast. Breakfast was oatmeal, raison bran and pancakes and two cups of coffee. Can't remember whom I ate with. Came back to the low with the Times in my arm, glanced at it and went to sleep till ten. By ten woke up and wandered into Sam's room and read some Gaugin and listened to Beethoven's fifth. We had no work group because Mrs. Stevens was out this week. Got dressed for my D. A. combed my hair for discipline's sake and went. Hello! Then a retelling of what i've been writing all the good things and then asked if Sue and Deb could come on Sunday. Dr. Plaut asked me to describe them and i almost went blank. How can I describe two people who are part of my life (though not a very large part)—I realized that I knew very little other than that Deb is working now and writing and Sue is going to Cooper [*Union*] and danses in her room and has acne. She allowed them. But I didn't tell her about Phil's coming this tomorrow. Tomorrow afternoon I have a pass to go out and that means that I'll probably see a movie with the folks. Sunday morning Deb and Sue, and Sunday afternoon I left open for aunt esther and uncle jack. I wish gabe [*Esther and Jack's son*] were back, he is really great and I laughed with him the Sunday he came. I respect him very much and would like to keep up a friendship if possible, what with the age differences and different mentalities—his a mathematical mind and mine a dansing poetical fancy, but there is hope—he did say he wanted to come back and so I'll take him by his word.

I asked the dr. if it was all right for me to masterbate and she said it was quite natural—calmed down some and maybe someday soon i will throw away that final layer of scum called guilt. Dr. also told me that she won't be here next week and that I would have a Dr. Franklin. I didn't think much of this other than it means that I stay in the hospital most likely one week longer. She asked me some family history and I told her about mother's side of the family and that I was close to aunt evelin, the dog, and madeline. Also tried to work out when grandma and grandpa died but my memory was muffled.

Went to lunch and had a fish plate with kind of tasteless halibut and a chicken sandwich and then a tunafish sandwich. Again don't remember whom I had dinner with. Now i remember—Georgia Britt. We talk a walk after lunch and then went to the canteen, she bought me a crakerjacks and some charms and we lingered awhile—the conversation escapes me, except that she said I reminded her of four of her previous boyfriends, which I took as a compliment. She made some statement about how silly it was for any couple to go steady here, being that they were both sick and I agreed. One of us also said that they would miss so much. I think we are both getting interested in each other and want to warn each other so. Finished Gaugin's Intimate Journals with a smile. He really had some sense of humor, but now eight hours later I can't remember anything too well—he claimed that it was not a book just one man's opinions. The drawings on facing pages were quite good and inspiring. I'll get short breathed here because I want to watch The Twilight Zone—be back in half an hour.

Am back—The Twilight Zone starred Andy Devine in a tale about a tall tailer who gets welcomed by some men from outer space. I shall probably dream about it tonight. After finishing the book i phoned up mom and told her to come tomorrow afternoon so that we can go out somewhere. Then I went to U. N. class. It was interesting. I then talked to Shirley Stein—we talked about going back to college and she was quite depressed and i quite optimistic, for a change. Then I ate. We had roast with bows and potato. I sat with Sam then Larry and then Bob and Helen. I upset Helen becaunse I was so cheerful and wanted her to be—she resented it. Came back and played three games of ping pong with Billy F- Something won one. Then went visiting with beautiful Cindy. Was told I had a phone call and it was Sue. She'll come with Deb and Raphael Sunday hurrah. Then I called up Alex Seligman—he'll be

I wish gabe were back…I respect him very much and would like to keep up a friendship if possible, what with the age differences and different mentalities— his a mathe- matical mind and mine a dansing poet- ical fancy…

here Sunday afternoon with Rich double hurrah. I can hardly wait to see Rich, who knows what will happen all I know is that I love him and Pat very much and have right reason to. Went back to Cindy and Cookie and we taked about Amy Baron, Cindy's roommate—she speaks in riddles and is quite disorientated. Then we all went to the night's activity which was a Talent Show. When it was all over and they were having a curtain call Amy walked across the stage—it was very funny. Then I came back to the ward, watched part of Route 66 and started writing this. I feel as though this is getting to be a drag and will have to do some thing to liven it up. Now i'll do some reading maybe time space and architecture.

Saterday april 14, 1962 ten to ten

saterday is over and i have lots to tell. Woke up quarter to nine and so missed breakfast—played some ping pong and then welcomed aunt evelin and uncle paul. Spent an enjoyable morning with them. Showed them around the hospital and explained what i was doing and how i was getting better. Played aunt evelin a game of ping pong to show off and she almost beat me. Then we played some casino. Paul passed a computer test and so will be transferring to a new department come june. Steven [*Paul and Evelyn's son*] is going to get some award and i told them i felt steven creeping up on me. They asked what they could get for my birthday and I told them paints, so they will get me red blue and yellow—wow. Had three lunches: meat loaf cauliflower and potato and a meat ball sandwhich and then for dessert plums. Talked with Roz—can't remember who else. Went back to the ward with a terrible headache which i had since i woke up. Took some aspirins and tried to relax.

My parents arrived and we left for a movie. We saw a Billy Wilder movie entitled "One Two Three" about a coco-cola plant in West Germany. It was amusing but nothing as funny as "Some Like it Hot "or "The Apartment." Went out afterwards for sundaes—had a marshmellow sundae and an english muffin. Returned just in time for dinner which was quite lousy. Brought back lots of presents for my birthday. Three prints to put on the walls—a Picasso clown, a Utrillo scene and "Indian Story" by Klee. Also a little iron horse which is hansome. Wandered around afterwards looking for people but everyone seemed occupied—Bob was writing, or rather typing, Cindy was sketching, Norman Fried was off in the woods getting drunk and Sam was out on a pass. So I wandered around looking at clouds and silloettes of trees pretty lonely. Finally spoke with Cindy and she read some of her poems and haikus so i said i would read her some of mine.

Wandered around afterwards looking for people but everyone seemed occupied... So I wandered around looking at clouds and silloettes of trees pretty lonely.

Came back to the low and found the cookies that Phil had left (forgot to mention that Phil came in the afternoon while I was gone. I phoned him and we had almost nothing to say to each other—telephones are dastard things) and the little horse. We went into the conference room and i had all to do to not touch her so beautiful body. She started dancing and i felt beauty. I got kicked out and came back to the ward and watched Perry Mason which had its usual stuff. Then went to the autotorium for the dance and danced wildly with Cindy and i could feel the look of the patients on us but i soon forgot them and we almost flew—we danced about three wild songs and each was tired no end.

Listenend in to a conversation between Bob and an artist girl who just came last week. She is quite pretty around 25 and has been hanging around with mr. Fazzio whom i would say is near his sixties. The realationships in this hospital are quite extraordinary. I chimed in about discipline and how necessary it is. Like coming my hair and getting to things that I have been talking to Dr. Plaut about. I took a walk under the stars and got a pop then watched a trial show in which the defendant declared himself guilty and i remembered trying to kill my father and Dr. Bolker and Tom's wife—I felt guilty to say the least. Talked with Sam about not leaving the premises and he asked me if i was lecturing him, i said i was lecturing myself. Then came to the room to type this. Tomorrow should be a good day. Now i'll go to Marty's room for some music and talk.

Sunday April 15, 1962

Woke at a quarter to nine. Washed and got dressed—called for my medications. Nine twenty saw Marna out in the hall. And I do love her and I don't know what I am going to do? Nothing—wait till she comes. Called my friends are here, Sue and Deb. We go to the conference room. I put on my grey shirt and tie. Sue brought out all sorts of pictures, about Chartres cathedral and a print by Klee and some walt kelly cartoons. We talked, Sue played some bach on the piano we talked about what? Who knows or cares. Deb looked ravishing—she has long hair now instead of the butch hair-cut she used to have and new glasses. She read her poems—most of them were occasion poems and they were reasonable. I read my three haikus—they liked them. Then i played on the piano emerson [*college*] style the way i used to play with Kevin [*in California*]. Then it was time for them to go.

Ate lunch with Marna and Bob Gold, again what did we talk about o yeah the fact that Jill was coming—I said i was nervous she said she knew how I felt. Then she said she saw Pat and she thought she was mainlining—I asked what—that she was taking H. Shit—so I cross off Pat now from my list of friends just like that you say goodby to a beautiful friend so maybe it isn't so.

Marna gets kicked out of the dining room and Bob gives her money to bring back sundaes. I wander around the ward, go play some more of my music for Roz, and Pat Barber, we laugh and have fun. Someone says someone is looking for me. I go out and find Marna and Raphael sitting under the sataircase—she has lots of carvel and I bring one up to Bob—he is sitting on his bed with a hermes typewriter on his lap typing captials. I come down and we smooze a bit, Raphael is still stealing books and as uncommunica-tive as always but he is beautiful and brilliant.

We take a walk to cottage x and sit around there for a while, then to the dining room for some coffee. Shirley Steinberg joins us and we talk again about what Tillie is wearing—a dress she made herself and talks on and on about how fat she is. We leave and come to the low lobby.

Aunt Esther and uncle jack come. I kiss them and bring every-one in to see my paintings—everyone loves my new paintings and can see the improvement over my earlier ones. I am very proud. Mrs. August comes in and says I can only have two visitors. Marna starts yelling and Mr. Elder escorts her and Raphael to the gate. Show aunt and uncle about—we talk about me getting better and learning bridge and about Gabriel and Lea [*their daughter*] and Bo [*Lea's husband*] and david [*Lea and Bo's son*] and jingo their dog. We take a walk around and have some more coffee. Both of them ask three times if they have to tip the chef for giving us coffee—just like "outsiders"—they always have to pay for everything—nothing for nothing is their motto.

Return in the hope that al and jill are coming. We go to the conference room and talk about negroes and how nice it is to have a nice family that one can get along with. Nearing three thirty and they want to leave. Escort them to the door and they thank me for the good time they had. Both remarked as usual about what a place it is.

Go upstairs and visit with Bob. He takes out some scrolls in chinese and explains them to me. He is just like William Sayroyan. I relax and tell him that I am learning how to relax—he approves no end and says there is no reason to be miserable. We talk about the people who come to visit me being sick, and I am getting better. That when when I was in california.—I had nothing in my head but now that wouldn't frighten me. Talk about my plans. Either an analyst, in movies and make my money in real estate or a kibbutz where I can bring up my children. He tells me not to get married for a few years and then marry a woman I can handle maybe two or three years at least younger than I. I told him about Dan Keller telling never marry a woman who admires you because someday she loses the admiration. And I wonder if he was on H. And then I remember John Gates and the time when we all three were sitting in the kitchen of Dan's house at point lobos just sitting and talking and when I pick my head up and am handed a joint as if from nowhere, and jazz playing on and on and me getting higher and higher and smelling the pine and cypress and what a fool i was to think that there were things or people in new york that I missed. Well I've got another chance now and I'll go to berkeley to get an education—a scientific one and then can be free again after analysis.

We talked about being strong and independent and art and I was glowing because once again I was in touch with a human being.

Then we went to dinner, Billy (Siegel) was waiting there sad with a hangover so I talked with him and the lighting outside was almost religious. And he said i was a good kid and, almost blushed. Once again I was proud only this time I knew I deserved it and know now that I am pretty good. We had greasy chicken with luscious sweet potato and mixed vegetables. Ate had sweet potato and sour cream and plums for dessert. Then sat with Larry Bob Selig and Cindy came in a little later. Talked about Larry's gai friend and how she was adjusted and I wondered why the morbid preoccupation in this place about homosexuality. And i know I'm not just projecting. Then sat with Roz and Gary then we went for a walk and kidded Roz about her bosim and that we wanted to have

We talked about being strong and independent and art and I was glowing because once again I was in touch with a human being.

an Orgy (Notice the capitalization) so we walked a little in the woods and then it started to snow so we came in. Saw Bob and had him (Siegel) put up the picasso and utrillo with me. Then we went to visit Cindy and so to the movie. Simpson (a nurse) told me there was a call for me and that I should call back. It was Sid and he had gotten screwed up with his chick and Rich hadn't even called him. I spoke to Don also and then cut the conversation short like my doctor wants. Went to the movie "Somebody Up there Likes Me"—the Rocky Graziano story. About a poor east side kid who grows up to be the middleweight champion. They had a feedback noise through the whole movie. There was one scene that I had to walk out on. The mother came to visit him in jail and she talked about her worrying and getting shock treatments etc it was too close to home and Bob S. and I both walked out. We both came back and the movie wasn't that bad. Saw Roz very depressed and tried to talk to her. Told her she had to go to all her activities and not withdraw—she got better and I didn't know whether to kiss her good night or not. didn't. Tomorrow is monday and a new week in another day I'll be nineteen hoorah and so what, the world is still with us.

o how i hate people who rape trees

something there is that doesn't love a neighbor

Monday April 16, 1962 ten o'clock

wee! what a wonderful day. Just took a shower painted another picture and am listening to some good music—all is right with the world. This typewriter ribbon is going but another tape is coming from home, all my needs except one are taken care of that one is sex. Woke at a reasonable hour went to the dining room and washed there then had an enormous breakfast: two cereals, two juices, coffee and pancakes. Talked with Phyllis Helen and Bob. Came back and tried to sleep o how luscious is some extra rest. Went to O.T. and painted a table and a bedstand. Enjoyed the painting for the first time. Mrs. Stevens with all hair was back and she asked what we would like to plant on the farm. Had coffee and cleaned up early. Forget what lunch was oh yes it was london broil with broiled tomato—ate with the twins and Roz ate an apple returned to the low and then went back had a sanwich and talked with some one, the weather was nice bought a cigar and newspaper and went to volleyball. Played a game of ping pong with little mr. marcus and I did not let pity win him the game—then I played volleyball. Two games i served good but how long can you play volleyball even in a good "mileau" so I went to the library to read a book on Rosseau le dounier, how meticulous he was o if i could paint like that with green details he must have loved green he must have loved the world. Mr. bright caught me so I had to return to the auditorium. Read some of the newspaper and then returned to the low in time for a conference with mr. Arms and the wakeup committee. Boy how people can talk about nothing.

Went to Sam's room since it was too late to go to sight reading and painted a picture the medium i used was oil and india ink. I made three stick figures on a field of brown and blue. It resembles a picture by klee. Went to dinner. Ate with Larry, Bob S. and Pat— joked as usual and then Larry's roommate Kate came and I had a chicken salad sandwich and the pot roast also got some sour cream and it tasted a little like beef stronganoff. Took a walk with Candy who looked much better than last night and kissed her. We ended up in one of the cottages but I decided I'd go to the poetry meeting. Cindy sat across from me, beautiful Cindy did. Helen and Bob and Billy were there. We read some cummings and frost. Left to see a green sunset which was beautiful. The clouds were what I think are called cumulous—they were big and spread around. What majesty what joy.

Returned to the ward and got dressed for a social we were to have with cottage x. Went there, dansed some cha cha and some folk danses, escaped with Sam Ware and went to low 2 but got thrown out. First however we got to kiss Cindy. Came back to the ward and took my second shower since i've been here. The water was like needles and then little relaxors it was great and I got clean scrubbing out the underarm and testicles smell. Did a wash and painted another picture and then came here to type.

A simple day but a better one. I am am gaining discipline and enjoying the simple things, learning how to talk to people and what not to say, to keep quiet and listen. Craking some jokes because I feel like not to attract attention the way I used to. Will read some jimanez who is beautiful. Only two pages tonight i am getting better all the time.

Tuesday April 17, 1962

today i was nineteen wow—it is just another day but i am older and i know that but what? So I received some nice burthday cards, a shirt from aunt ethel—it is very handsome it has silk embroidery. Another poem from aunt pearl and her style is beginning to give. A poem from Cindy (and Amy whom i think is getting better) along with a birthday card and a birthday card from Candy. Slept naked last night and it felt good—got a little wet but I have asked my doctor and i was almost told that I was a fool to doubt that i could and should masterbate. Woke early had a big breakfast with Sam and mrs. Lewis (a nurse) and she is very nice. Ran back to the ward for the feel of my pillow and some sleep. Constantly nagged by the staff and then told that I had an appointment with dr. Franklin at nine-45. Went in my blue sweatshirt and talked for a half hour just general stuff. Said I missed dr. Plaut but know that she'll return next week and so am not worried. Was able to be free with him and liked him. I'll have another appointment with him this week.

Then the rorshock tests. I kept insisting that they were only ink-blots and that it was a crime to make them anything else.

Went looking for the bridge class but there didn't seem to be one. Tried to read time space and architecture but became immensely hungary. Went to lunch and had corn beef hash with the twins and roz. Then with bob s. and we went to the commisary and he is a very sweet guy. Pretty sensitive and smart and well built. I had an appointment with Dr. Bach the psychologist, started at 12:45 and finished after four. He gave me a whole battery of tests. Started with me reproducing some simple geometric shapes. Then he made me draw them from memory. I did pretty well. Then some questions like what would I do if there was a fire in a theatre and I said look for the nearest exit fire extinguisher and the manager then see if i could help him. Why is land cheaper in the country then in the city—supply and demand—what would you meaning me, do if I was lost in the forest—look for the sun—what if i found a sealed stamped addressed envelope—drop it in a mail box. Then some simple arithmetic questions. Then he asked me to draw a tree, a house and a man and a woman.

Then the rorshock tests. I kept insisting that they were only ink-blots and that it was a crime to make them anything else. I found about five things however which he never heard or saw before which made me quite proud. Then the thematic aperception test. I'll try and remember what I gave.

A picture of a boy drooped over a violin. "He is dreaming that he is playing at carnegie hall when two men accost him (I called them foreign aids!) he plays some strange music they disappear and his girlfriend floats down from one of the boxes they live happily ever after."

2. A girl looking forlorn with a farm scene in back of her. "She has just been told that she would make a good dr. but who ever heard of a woman dr. and anyway the needed her on the farm, her widowed mother and brother. Her brother hears however and puts her through medical school where she dies in the last year from lung cancer because she smoked too much while studying."

3. A boy sleeping and fatherly figure looking at him. "the father a cobbler is looking at the boy who is dreaming of bringing up his family on a kibbutz"

4. A man with arms around him. This is K who is about to die like a dog. He lives in constant fear and guilt and anxiety the way most people live. It is too bad that he lived in an age prior to psychioanalissis and so he is consumed by his own feelings.

6. A man with his arm over his head is standing by the bedside of a naked woman. "The man is the family doctor who is about to remove one of the breasts of the woman because she has cancer. He does and doesn't tell anyone that she has only a few months to live. She lives on however and brings up her three children and lives happily ever after."

7. A girl on a bridge. "She is about to jump when the long-shoremen down below invite her in for a game of bridge. She plays with them and realizes that she has what to live for. When she leaves Lennie follows her rapes her then stabs her. Her friend Jim Steel writes her story and wins a pulitzer prize. He drinks himself to death however since he has lost the only thing or being he has ever loved.

I think that is all. Then he gave a sentence completion test. I admire most—I put in bob gold. My mother—loves me very much.

I am tired now and shall probably read and do some talking from now on I am a man in his last year as a teen.

I went back to the low introduced myself to the new patient Jim Frost and picked up a card from roz and from Cindy. Played lots of Ping Pong with Bill Morris and then went to dinner. Had dinner with Bob S. Bob Gold and Ilsa and Phyllis. It was stew and not so good. Then went to choral group with that horribly effeminate gladstone as the instructor. Why my wrath over effeminency? Probably because I fear it in myself. I shall try however to unleash my feminine traits through love and my arts. Then went to playreading and was bored by the importance of being earnest. Made one good line—Oscar was describing relations as ugly creatures whom one endured and I added 'on weekends.'

Then came back to the ward. Found some pictures by picasso in a time and hung them on the wall. Forgot that earlier i stopped into the library and picked up a copy of the koran and stole a copy of colette. If only i could read i would be ecstatic but the thorazine blurs my eyes. I am tired now and shall probably read and do some talking from now on I am a man in his last year as a teen.

wednesday april 18, 1962

At the government meeting on the low, Bill, the president, said something about having our affairs (the birthday party for the whole hospital) being successful. I bantered back hadn't you better keep your affairs private for only you and your doctor?

another day and am I getting better? A watched pot never boils or it takes longer and what I learned from zen about how not to press issues i am now unlearning by watching and having professionals watch. But I do want to get better and start having a good time and fulfill my potential, etc. Today i woke up early in my nidoty, clothed myself washed and went off to breakfast. Came back, slept some more and then had to change my linen—have a beautiful new pillow case. Slept some more and then went to the clinic to let the vampires or technicians take some of my blood. Wandered into the library—glanced through a book of graphics from the expressionists, and then a book on michelangelo. Went to o.t. but mrs. stevens wasn't there—wandered around some more—had my first piece of matzo. did some painting and then checked out. Did not feel guilty about not working felt as if I knew what I was doing. Made up my mind not to come to work tomorrow. Came back, picked up all my birthday cards from daddies family—no money—disappointed. Went to lunch had fish. Helen said i was the king of the non-sequitor. Both Bobs were there. am seeing the whole bob gold now not just my adulation and he still stands up as a pretty great fellow. Helen was laughing for about the third time i've seen her do that and I felt that I was in good company.

Walked back by myself and looked at the Times and then went off to sleep. again slept till about two then decided to read tom sawyer and started reading it. Then went to the government meeting at which as usual nothing much happened. Played some ping pong, got dressed, ironed my shirt but wore the shirt aunt ethel gave me—it has a nice embroidered pattern and it is a very silky cotton. Got dressed for the sedar and went.

First called mother to wish her a happy pesach and she decided to give me a lecture. Said the doctors said i was very sick and that I had too many friends on the week end i told her to stop it and we both hung up. I know i'm sick probably better than anyone it is me who feels un free and depressed and inferior and slightly paranoid nobody else, it is me who finds it hard to sit still and concentrate. It is I who haven't been able to communicate with people what the hell is she complaining about. I am perfectly honest with the doctors and my parents what do they want it takes time and more time. It took how many millions of years to produce me and my environment I can't get well overnight.

Went to the sedar—a rabbi officiated and he said only the kiddush the four questions and daianu—that was the sedar!—had a full meal. Wine, which I only had a few drinks since I am on thorazine and feared getting sick, chorazis and horse radish. Gefulte fish, soup, chicken, carrot and potato and i was getting nervous i don't know why. bob said it probably reminded me of my family and that I wanted to be with them.

I took a walk outside and back to the low where all the people who felt too sick to go to the sedar were. Well I knew I wasn't that sick so I decided on going back. Had lots of pineapple and two oranges some cake and then took a walk with bob and helen. Went to visit cindy and candy and cindy was in her pajamas not going to the dance. Candy said she wasn't going either. Candy wanted me to play dominoes with her. She taught me the game and I won two Went to the dance and met a new girl, very pretty, from Miami, named Doris. Talked with her for a while then dansed with heather but got no enjoyment out of dansing—tried to remember what my first day was like and remembered how nervous and anxious I was. I had a pack of cigars which I was smoking and played scrabbel that night with john, helen, bob and phyllis. Bob drew my picture and I drank four cups of coffee. I didn't sleep that night but read some of Milne's Chloe Marr. That was three or four weeks ago. Tried to talk with Marty and Sam but they were aludding to parts of the conversation that I hadn't been part of—most annoying. Sandy, looking gorgeous, asked me if i told Sam (Ware) how I felt about him, i said no, he probably wouldn't understand, and then I said I didn't really feel that strongly (homosexual) about him, just that he was very attractive. Came back to the low and started writing.

thursday

I came to sandy's cottage in the rain and i was wearing my trenchcoat—she said i looked like i was from the fbi—where were my credentials? so i picked up my shirt and showed her my belly button.

Thursday april 19, 1962

Slept lushously till ten with lots of interuptions, aids waking me up for medication and women coming in telling me I had to go to work group but I merrily said it was pesach and I don't have to work on passover. They agreed so i finally got up a little hungary and tried to read some tom sawyer but my heart was not with it. looked at the times, washed and showed some people how to play korean solitaire which I learnt from mr. snow when I was at elmhurst [hospital]—I haven't written anyone and I should. Went to lunch and had veal parmigian and three ice creams—ate with susan and we laughed watching the doctors eat. One of them was very effiminant and ate very very slowly.

Came back to the low and waited for a while, can't remember what I did, then went out into the beautiful weather, gigantic massive white clouds and spots of pure blue. Tried to draw the daffodills and tulips and hyacinths but didn't do a very good job. then went out and sang "once i had a candy store" to the tune of hatikvah with Billy and phyllis and susan—we all sang different words and it was fun. Then helen phyllis and i played scrabble on their low. I had to leave at two for a doctors appointment. It went very quickly and I got a pass for this saterday. I talked for the whole half hour and mentioned my "anxiety" if that was what it was last night and the fact that I am getting bored with people again.

I went back to the library and glanced at a book of Miro's—o what colours stark reds, blues and yellows why didn't i ever think of that—then a book on american indians and then a book of the posters of the french school: picasso, braque, chagall, miro, dufy

went out into the beautiful weather, gigantic massive white clouds and spots of pure blue… sang "once i had a candy store" to the tune of hatikvah with Billy and phyllis and susan—we all sang different words and it was fun.

and matisse—great colours again and i saw some composition i returned to the low (it is called low after a lowenstein who must have given a lot of money—they have a horrid portrait of him out side in the lobby) and proceeded to paint like miro i made a sun sky and red and yellow flowers but it didn't look too good—then I went over the first picture i did here with some blue (it had two suns with some blue red and green). (the radio is playing stravinski's firebird and it is the way i felt today walking under the steel sky—spring) 1) Then i took an impression of the blues on some paper and fooled around a bit. It was by then after 4:15 andi met bob and he said let's do something exciting. I felt the same way so we walked around and it was raining glorious. We decided on picking up sandy and the anecdote that I told earlier happened. Had liver with sour cream and sat with sam, he claiming still to be a vegetarian, had a salad plate. We hardly talked—then bob and candy came—we sang some songs and had a good time. Candy said she might be able to get some pot and my eyes lit up. Had coffee with bob, helen and phyllis and asked how phyllis was—she had come back last night after her first day out in nine months. She was scared on the subway and didn't complete the college tests that she went for—she said she was a little better. And helen was wonderful she was laughing again and it was good to see her laughing. went back and stopped in on the science class and said I was looking for my raincoat. Bob had brought it back. Went to get susan but found cindy first. Rather i found the new girl marge—she is quite boehmian looking, petite and had a stack of klee postcards so now there is another girl for me. Amy baron slammed her door and marge jumped—there was nothing i could do she was quite upset. Then we went into the conference room and talked with cindy. We talked about the psycho tests and marge said she had been going through pyshoanlysis five times a week. We discussed some further things and then I read cindys first scene to a play she is writing—it was alright but nothing special—a lot of projecting. I analyzed as usual.

Marty came in and marge left for a scrabble game. Marty is getting very morbid and philosophical about death and I sound like a school teacher protesting that life is worthwhile and once we have been anylized not a nightmare as it is for most persons. He sounded just like i would sound off after reading kafka or camus and this time i was the optimist and it felt good. We left and i found Bob Gold sitting in the hall—we talked for a while and then I asked him if he would like to see my new paintings. He came and loved them, smiling, he gave me a big hug and wanted the one with the three people in black. I was very honoured. Billy (Siegel) and Jim Frost were there and they also said they like the pictures. I was happy because I had created something that other people enjoyed and could understand.

I have life
and then
some—painting
and some
poetry and
people—who
could ask
for more?

Then I went to the teen lounge with Frost and did a few of my wild dances—started jumping up and down with marty—it was great fun and of course they tried to stop us, so I went to the adult lounge knowing that mr. arms (group worker) wouldn't be there, and played some monopoly in place of helen and bob. Billy took over bobs hand and immediately started bargaining—he is so brilliant. He took my park place to make a monopoly and promised me immunity, 400 dollars and the next property that I needed. he said it was the only way to beat the two girls and he was right.

Played some ping pong with bob s. and then with some guy named Peter—I won some of the games and then candy came. We walked back and I got to kiss her goodnight. Forgot to mention that I called up alan and muriel [*cousins*] before I went to teen lounge—she asked about the flowers and I asked if Alan had been writing—a question that took guts to ask. She said on and off. They will call me when they can come. I love them very much and I really can't explain—they are two very healthy people and were always very kind to me. I think I am getting better—at least I am able to feel things again. I am happy for most of the time, so things are looking up. I have life and then some—painting and some poetry and people –who could ask for more?

needles of pine piercing the silver domed sky
fluttering

Friday april 20, 1962

Woke up early today after a mixed up dream—it had me working for Victor Kayvets, the hospital, Berkeley and several other of my existences in it. Went to breakfast and had some horrible eggs. Read the newspaper and talked with candy. came back, cleaned up the room—my bed is now under the window and makes a studio arrangement, leaving lots of space in the middle. Went to individual o.t. but first met sy who is living on low 3 and wants to make friends with me. He stutters, is fairly good looking and seems somewhat smart—complimented me on my dancing last night, said that there was a long scroll-like package for me in the package room. I walked there with him and picked up a long tube (just took about three quarters of an hour out to talk with alan so may not have enough time to finish tonight) and wanted to open it up there but somehow i constrained myself and came back to the low.

There were two beautiful little pictures one a picasso a blue boy up against roses and another was a Kandinsky and then there was a big poster from mexico—the walls are beginning to get covered and it is looking nice. Went to o.t. and started wedging clay to throw it. Finally got around to working on the potters wheel—whee what fun! the hands get full of slip and the cylinder starts to form as if by magic and it is great. Of course it being the first time something would go wrong and it got a tremendous airpocket.

By then it was time for lunch—had blue berries and crème instead of fish—ate with William and some of his friends. Then i went walking came back to the low played ping pong with someone or other and then i went back to o.t. to read a book on ceramics. Read the book and got a little inspired—want very much to work in clay—it was a good feeling to be connected with earth and not just words or colors. Went to the library and started reading a book called the five colour method by Donnie Rudnik's uncle. Bob S. came in and said that was the book he wanted to read. I read some and then got blurry again, I hate when that happens i think i fear going blind like dad [*our father was blind in one eye, legally blind in the other*]. Stayed around outside the pavillion and talked with helen and bob and carrie. Went with bob and we talked some and then went to dinner around five so that we could meet cindy, we didn't so ate with bob and helen. Bob S. got annoyed because bob said he could teach me all about colours and that certain colours were necessary. We then visited cindy and marge and didn't talk much. marge had a marlboro box on the table and I asked if i could make an obscene joke—she said yes and i said she had a nice box.

Candy came and we took a walk—candy, bob, gary another girl and me. Forgot to say we stoopped in before supper and saw sandy and read some psychological articles, one that said pyshoanalysis should be replaced with socioanalaysis and that the kids peer group was much more important to an american group than his relation to father—very interesting, only i got the time mixed up—did that after we walked and went to a softball game. Bob and alan got in but I didn't—enjoyed watching everyone play specifically like the field when the teams were coming in off the field and going out after—have to stop. stopped last night because the aids complained that some of the patients were disturbed and that I was disturbing them.

Didn't do much else yesterday—went up to the auditorium with bob s. and did an indian leg wrestle with him, then came back to the low because they were having games again. Wanted to stay near bob because he looked so confused and mixed up and angry. Read some tom sawyer and talked to him—did not help much but he drew and got less angry. I came back to my room and started writing when gary came in—we threw the bull around and i tried to encourage him that he should do things. He is terribly tence and about the only thing he seems able to do is play cards and sleep. He's a bright guy and i like him but hardly ever get a chance to do anything with him. Bob dropped in and then I stopped typing. Alan stayed awhile—I washed up and called it a night but had a hard time getting to bed i guess i was a little anxious about today, going out with the family.

Saterday April 21, 1962

Got up fairly early, went to breakfast, ate with some and excused myself, wanting to get back to that luscious pillow—did and slept till ten when i was wakened by Mrs. August, saying that I had company—who could it be? it was my father coming around early before meeting the doctor. We talked some and then I walked him to the doctors office—we planned on seeing "Two Women" this afternoon. walked around and saw some people lounging in the back yard—the weather was beautiful so i stayed awhile but got scared that I would burn.

Came inside and covered myself with the suntan lotion—just got told off again by billy siegel and wanted to slam him one but refrained and clammed up and was silent which is the worst thing i could do but did as usual. He upsets me because I respect him—no, am afraid of his "wisdom" which in the final analysis is probably no greater than mine.

I went into Donnie Rudnik's room to see how he was (he had early in the evening, I was told, first collapsed and then thrown a fit, after which Dr. Plaut came in from her vacation to take care of him and Maryse and Payne went upstairs and did I don't know what to him)—he was quite logical and talkative and then Billy walked in and immediately demanded his attention and I said something about his being black and white and not middling and or able to compromise and immediately he jumped at me with words that who was i to know anythng about him i was just a little schmuck.

Donnie tried to come to my defence and after a while billy said he had something personal to say to Donnie and i decided to leave and donnie called out i was a nice boy, which cheered me up some so i spit and that was how my anger went, if it has. But it has for i must remember that people here are sick and therefore use others to remain sick and sometimes their sensitivities become quite bald if that analogy can hold any water, but I'll get back to the narration of the day since that is my responsibility and i guess escape.

> He upsets me because I respect him— no, am afraid of his "wisdom" which in the final analysis is probably no greater than mine.

Billy was lying on a chair and susan and her mother were also sitting there and they wanted me to bring out my paintings but i did not feel like exhibiting myself so said I was getting too burnt. Thorazine is a great excuse for so many things.

Went up to the auditorium but first heard that dr. franklin was looking for me and that I couldn't have alan come tomorrow afternoon or gil wax. So I called him up and he sounded a little left out and i was but i must follow doctor's orders. Right now I don't seem to want to continue i want to save my face and go back there and beat him up—real physical violence but 1. he is stronger than me, 2. what would i gain and three i have a job that I usually enjoy to do, so I'll be sencible.

Went up to the auditorium and played a game of volley ball, our side lost and I left. Hung around the low and went to lunch i can't remember who with o no it was with bob s. and we had roast beef he didn't like the meal but I rather liked it. Left, saw the weeping cherry, fell apart, and played someone ping pong. Then saw marty and roz and took a walk with them to the woods—they had a blanket waiting in the middle of a bunch of pine and it was really beautiful. I smelled the pine and sky and just lay there completely relaxed.

Came back at 1:45 and dressed so that i could go out with the parents. Met dad in the waiting room and we drove to nassau county and saw "Two Women" and "Ballad of a Soldier" (for my third time). "Two women" was good and gave a sence of the violence and destruction that war brings to/brought to the italian people and specifically a woman and her girl. The girl was great and sophia loren acted as if she were a mannikan, I thought. "Ballad" was kind of corny but my throat got a little caught near the end and mother was in tears. They wanted to take me to a soda place and I kept saying it was passover. We stopped in a place but first I stopped into an army navy store and bought a pair of black jeans—"wee jeans"—I felt mixed about asking the parents for money but also felt that i deserved it. Then we had cokes and I saw a book called "how I made a million in real estate" but somehow the parents dissuaded me. Came back and then they showed me the oils and brushes they had bought for me. I kissed them both goodby and thanked them for a nice day which it really was.

Came back and met Cindy—asked her to wait and then to see my pictures—she did but got thrown out. Went to dinner with cindy and bob (he came back for a recource) and bob and helen and phyllis listened to some conversation while eating the hamburgers neatly disengaging them from the buns. Cindy and I had an argument in nonsense talk. Came back and then went for a walk with bob s. Met Bob and Helen on the basketball court and played some. Spent the rest of the time watching some baseball practice and then going up to low three's sun porch. I said it was wonderful to watch their relationship grow and mature and got laughs. helen remarked that I had my own way with flirting with about twenty girls on the grounds, after I said hello to someone. Sat up on the porch and bob sang some deepthroated russian songs. Left them to visit helen and marge and did. Big jack was there and we discussed traveling around the country. He's done almost everything. Went to the nights activity with helen and met bob up there. Tried to dance with helen and then cindy. Bob S. disappeared and I played a form of badmitton with larry. Saw candy who looked terribly upset (earlier in the day she walked right by me with her boy friend billy and i was quite insulted).

We played ping pong with a cracked ball and it was fun—commented how like life unexpected and all it was.

Played some whist but not enjoying it quite which is a good habit that I'm getting into, fucking doing things I don't enjoy. Talked with bob g. about not getting involved with the patients here and he asked if i blamed him for getting involved with helen and i said no and he said she was one of the most beautiful women he had ever met. I agreed. We played ping pong with a cracked ball and it was fun—commented how like life unexpected and all it was. Met candy and decided i would try and help her. Tried to get her to stop crying and it took me about a half an hour to get her to.

have to stop, it being past 11.

Sunday 22, april, 1962

had a beautiful day. The weather was in the 80's and I have just come in after running around wild out in the back. But I'll begin where i'm supposed to. Woke up after nine, went into the living room and started to watch television when I saw the sillowette of Sue. She came with deb and we went into the back yard and sat a while with phyllis and then helen. I came in to get clothed and lotioned and then wanted them to come into the conference room because i was afraid of the sun. Billy saw me and asked me to forgive him for last night—he had a bad temper he said. I did. I don't know what we talked about but the time fled and sue played some piano and I walked them to the gate—they won't come next weekend which is good. Give me some time to rest. Went to lunch—had k.p.—did it and then stayed around and listened to some woman who just came in last week. She had periods of elation and then depression in six month swings.

> We went to sit under the pines... We talked and didn't talk and it was very easy going...

It was 1:15 and i was expecting jay and dad but they didn't come so I laid down. About two thirty dad popped into the room and we talked some and waited for jay to come. He did. Straight from [*college roommate*] Arnie's wedding—they had a reformed rabbi take care of the ceremony in the home and then they left in a new volvo that someone gave them. We went to sit under the pines and I brought a blanket out and invited bob s. to join us—he did for a while and then left. We talked and didn't talk and it was very easy going, except that jay had forgotten to bring the canvasses. We went into the library and I showed dad a beautiful haggadah and I looked at a book about Giotto and his contemporaries. They came back for their coats and I took them to the back yard when I heard my name called. It was mother—she had come to bring the canvasses—I was overjoyed and didn't want them to leave but they had to.

Walked back and then went to an early dinner—ate with cindy, marge and bob s. We giggled a lot and then they went on k.p. Talked with a guy who said he was studying antrhopology at columbia, then bob and helen came to eat and i moved to their table. Talked and then they took a walk and I had to bring the milk and cookies back to the low—did that and joined them under the pines.

Bob asked me and I told them I couldn't see their relationship as ending anywhere short of marriage. Then we discussed marna as we had at the dinner table. About how unstable she is and how close to almost shrieking. And very near her limit—also talked about her wonderful father and miserable mother and helen said that the house was cold and I agreed and then we went up to the sun porch and sat till it got pink and then dark in time for the movie. It was the "Rainmaker" which I had seen a long time ago at the granada when jay was sick. I enjoyed it a great deal—thought kathren hepburn was good and lancaster also. Met candy afterwords and went for a walk in the heated night. Billy and susan came along and I asked them to leave and i was afraid that the pictures susan had brought for me from the museum of modern art would fly away but they didn't. Then I was afraid of whether or not to kiss or start to make love to candy. She said something about how much healthier i was because i was seven years her junior and that decided it for me. We got up and returned. Then I went into the back by climbing out my window and ran around with marty and sam and then I came to type. But I want to go talk so i'll finish here.

Monday april 23, 1962

it was an early night last night so I went to bed right afer writing—had a little hard time falling asleep so i played games as usual and got a little tired. Can't remember what I dreamed—woke up in time for a breakfast of sorts. Ate with Larry and someone else, then came back to sleep as usual. Woke in time for the rounds doctors and had nothing to say to them—told them i had an enjoyable weekend, which i did. Read some tom sawyer and then got ready to go to o.t. but there was none so i read some and then read the times pretty thoroughly—they had an hour by hour account of the hike in steel prices and i read that plus some other little things. Then it was time to see the "medical examiner" from the state.

We all lined up and I thought that as soon as we would say that the food was good they would stop serving us good food—it was in the "Grand Illusion" that something like that happened when the red cross would come around and they would give out blankets and things and here i associated for some reason and thought that I was really in a concentration camp, and somehow i was brainwashed to believe that it was for my own good. Went to lunch and forget what we had or whom i ate with—I am beginning to get lazy with you, little journal—no, I ate with bob s. it was corned beef with cabbage and i put mustard on them and was very hungary and had a salami sanwich i think. cindy joined us. Don't remember what I did between lunch and my doctors' appointment—played some ping pong, I think and then changed my pants and then went for the d.a.

Asked her if she had a nice vacation, apologizing for that type of question but curious. Discussed the weekend and then the quarrel with billy and how i refused to react. Was told that I'll get o.t. in the middle of may. Left the d.a. kind of happy because I talked what i wanted to. Made the dr. laugh. I made a long explanation on why I didn't go to work group on thursday and then i said i guess i felt that i was just getting out of work. Went to O. T. to see if I could help with the mural for the birthday party, but sam and bob were working on a small piece of paper so i wanted no part, I wanted a wall—went to the library and glanced at some picture books till 3, which was sight singing. My eyes were a bit blurry from the thorazine. Spent the three quarters of an hour there but felt as if i learned next to nothing—maybe i am too impatient with things but just singing do re mi fa soll la ti tol doesn't seem to teach me very much.

Met Bob s. in the library—he was copying from the book of posters I showed him and i started drawing in charcoll of the days' new york times. I also made three large sketches, one of a woman and man and then just a scribble. The man and naked woman are hanging over william's bed. Went to dinner with bob s. and had delisious potato pancakes with sour cream. Cindy joined us and i hopped from one table to another and bob d. had a potato pancake with us. Then some of the aids were rounding up a softball game so bob and i decided to join. Came back for all my sun shading. Played second base and got one strike out and two triples drove in two runs and missed one ball. Pretty good considering i haven't played for a few years. It was fun working on a team but i was tempted to quit and join the poetry reading but didn't.

Bob s. came in for some cheering up and we did, discussing our art and some of our mutual problems.

After it broke up went to the poetry reading on low 4 and they were discussing dylan thomas but i didn't hear very much of what they were saying. Came back to the low to see a special television show on picasso. Was almost tempted to send away for picasso's picassos and then never pay for it, but didn't—does that mean i am getting better? Viewing things as belonging to people instead of thievery and lying and get the best of authority figures etc. They turned it off in the middle because we were having low night and they wanted to have darts in the teevee room. I was quite annoyed and expressed my anger, but the show will be on on sunday also. Forgot to mention that after lunch we had a meeting of all those who find it hard getting up in the morning (punchline to a joke) and we will start to have callesthenics which is something to look forward to. I played a game of ping pong and was winning by a wide margin to Donnie but slowly lost the lead and then the game. Played some more later but lost all the games. Came in here to type after watching a half hour program on israel. Bob s. came in for some cheering up and we did, discussing our art and some of our mutual problems. I let it out that I did try to kill three people and he didn't believe it. He also liked my oil portrait (of myself) which i did earlier in the evening. Since then i have been writing now i stop.

We lived a life of adventure, there were three of us [*on Martense Street, where Robert and I grew up*], phil, marcia and i. Phil was the smartest of the threesome but i was the most adventursome and marcia was our fair lady who came along as good luck, and sometimes was the prize that we both fought for. They lived in a castle with winding staircases and i lived in a poor hut in the back of a small unit that housed four families, or what was left of four families.

daffodils are dying now lying in the sun

shriveling and powder turned done
I haven't spoken to anyone today
and yesterday is past
tomorrow will i remember how to speak?

tuesday april something or other 1962

did nothing today or next to it. Got up, went to breakfast, ate great or good griddle cakes, came back instead of going to some cookout and went to sleep. Was awakened for bridge but there was no bridge class so i went back to sleep—slept until 11:30, then went to lunch came back and went to sleep again. Then went to dance therapy and moved myself around a little, came back and slept till dinner—had a horrible dinner of fish and then played some ping pong and went to choral club. Sang a few songs, then returned to the low firs—meeting Marty and he is going crazy losing control of himself, giggling, talking endlessly so what am i supposed to do—just say another one gone i guess. He is sleeping now. Went into Sam's room and listenend to beetbottoms fifth, got inspired, did two paintings and then got my medications and am ready to get my diary in order and read some tom sawyer. Have hardly talked to anyone all day and do not feel as if I wasted it, the sleep was good and had lots of dreams mostly of my childhood i guess because of mark twain.

Went into
Sam's room
and listenend
to beetbottoms
fifth, got
inspired, did
two paintings
and then got
my medications
and am ready
to get my
diary in
order and
read some
tom sawyer.

just cheered bob up, he was talking about how is it that he is always asleep in his soul and it was like pulling teeth until he started smiling and then we talked some, about the hospital being a utopia, different people, and art. Got up by eight today, went to have breakfast and had some horrible eggs, bought a newspaper and read it instead of going to sleep. Came back and watched some television—"Amos and andy," also played some ping pong. Went to o.t. and read some jimenez, his poetry, wants to make me write poetry again but I am dry and the poetry would tell, so I'll wait. Did three things painted. Came back and finished getting my diary in order.

Went to lunch and had some roast i think with kashe varneskas, came back and did nothing, then went to the auditorium and played some volley ball. Went to the library and tried to study the five colour method but got blurry. Had an interesting session with my doctor. Started off complaining about having so little secondary sex characteristics and came around, with the doctor's help, to saying i am what i am. I made her laugh, once or twice. May get a pass tomorrow to get a haircut and go to the library. Talked about starting to study and i wanted to tackle everything at once as usual. Left very cheerful, went to the library in time to be told i was now on the library committee—sat through a boring meeting and then stayed, reading Time on DH Lawrence and a painter and then the five colour method.

Went to dinner but first stopped by the weeping cherry tree in front of the cottages—got detoured by a pretty girl—Laura. She was studying speed writing and I asked her if I could borrow her books—she said no, she needed them for reference but why don't I send away—they cost about 33 dollars. Well, I said something about never commiting myself and she said i had to commit myself to hillside and i agreed and certain other things. I read some of the

just cheered bob up, he was talking about how is it that he is always asleep in his soul and it was like pulling teeth until he started smiling and then we talked some, about the hospital being a utopia, different people, and art.

first book and the system seems reasonable—I will study it. Ate dinner with her and then bob and helen but they left early.

Had a delisous "matzo bry" and blueberries, then came back with laura and played two games of ping pong—I tried to win and did win, then we went up to the third low's sun porch where helen bob and kyle were. Kyle was telling some chemistry jokes about how one chemical was aided because the guys used to urinate in the vats and that when they made bigger vats it didn't work so they had to employ men to piss in them. Also about a guy who was driving a truck full of horse piss and got arrested and told the cop what he was carrying and got put in jail. He was a little manic, giggling and shouting.

At my D. A. told my doctor I didn't have to shout anymore but could say what i have to say and say it quietly. Then went to the birthday dance and refused to do my groucho marx routine because i thought i would make a fool of myself. First called up the folks and had a good conversation with them. Was bored with the dance—received a pen and pencil set for my april birthday. Danced a few of the dances and tried to talk to the new amy, but she was too cool for talk. She just sat behind her sunglasses (shades) and looked beautiful. I turned to candy and asked why don't we go into the woods. she liked the idea and we took a walk but nothing really happened. Looked at the clouds and they seemed to have tunnels of blackness surrounding them. The clouds had ice shapes to them. Came in and saw bob in bad shape with his bed undone (I left my dirty sheets on so that i wouldn't have to be bothered. So i tried talking to him and succeeded—it made me feel very good. That is all that happened today folks.

thursday april 26, 1962 one nine forty five

woke at eight after several nudgings. Ate cereals and juice and of cource coffee. Washed up in low bathroom. Bought a New York Times and tried to read it in the room. Spoke to dr. Plaut and she said i could probably go to the barber and library tomorrow. Read some hilarious tom sawyer. Went to O.T. and brought "the decline and fall of practically everybody," read about 25 pages, painted some furniture and then went looking for mother, who had an appointment at social servic- Was walking around the outside like a free man in his right mind. es. Was told i could not wait there so went downstairs and waited. A man came along, asked me if my name was robert—got a little scared but answered yes—he then asked me to guess his name. For some reason guessed sonny and I was right. He was a neighbor who took all my pictures and his wife susan used to work with or for dad. We talked and then mother came—he tried to get me to come to dinner but she wouldn't—afraid that she would break regulations. Finally said goodby to mother and had lunch with sonny. He is an insurance salesman and volunteered for the photography club which is very nice of him. I hope to get into the club.

Forgot to mention that i called rich. he sounded no different— was in a hassle again, needs a job to pay for his apartment—his father didn't pay for it after all. Wanted to come but told him I'd have to talk it over with my friend the doctor. He said he wanted to see me outa here soon and i agreed. Will recall him saterday. Showed Sonny my pictures and he liked some of them which means that i am doing something, probably not too radical. Took my medicine and put up a few more pictures—the room is beginning to look like home or a crazy house—most of the wall area is covered. Then waited for the government meeting and anticipated going on the bike ride. Went to visit cindy and had a nice visit. She is a very good girl. Came back and asked if i could go on a bike ride and was told no. I was kinna stunned. Asked to speak to my doctor and finally they did. She said i could go. Well i am starting to stand up for my rights. We were milling around—I went to change and put on my lotion and then we left.

Was walking around the outside like a free man in his right mind. Saw kids playing and they passed by not even noticing us. Got a shwinn bike instead of an english racer but was satisfied to have everything—rode around a little and then bought an ice cream sandwich—it's funny how you get to miss certain things. Rode to Alley pond park and was a little afraid of the traffic—got on the bike path and was last throughout the entire afternoon. It was fun but also hard work. I made an aforism saying that you can't coast all the time—sometimes you have to work. Relaxed for awhile and talked to the girls' social worker about her education and then stopped, not really being interested and just making small talk. Went back to the bike shop, paid my dollar and then went back to the luncheonette—first stopped into a supermarket for some cantelope but they were much too small. Had a vanilla malted with chocaolate ice cream. Stole one of those paddles with rubber ball attached. Then came back to the hospital and ate a supper with bob helen and phyllis—annoyed them with my toy. david called it neugeboren's masterbateur—then we went for a walk but I wanted so i came back to the low. Didn't want to go to science and it was called off so I went to sketching class, looked at a new book I borrowed called "Summerhill A radical approach to child rearing" by A. S. Neill. About an english school which believes in love not authority. Should be interesting (am i still being a diletante). Went to sketching an tried to sketch from a calendar—came out fair, did a carictiture of martha fleischer and it was pretty cute. Then just lazed around. Came back to the low and dressed up for the teen lounge they were going to have a live band there. Went and the band was composed of all brass, a drummer, a bassist, and two guitarists (electric)—they were young high school kids and on the loud side but it was live. Danced a few wild dances and one girl came over and asked me to do the next lindy with her. I felt proud. Fell down on the floor once and was out of breath another time, but my body was completely free—it was great. Like flying down the hill on the bike. Came back and met giggly candy—walked around a little with her, am becoming much freer with her and everyone else. The boys from low three teased me about pot. Came back to the low, played some ping pong and then came in to write the diary roger and out.

changed the ribbon [*on typewriter*] last night and it is much easier to read. Woke up around eight, had a good breakfast of french toast nad cereal. Came back and went to sleep—as usual got woken up to clean the room and did. Then read some of "Summerhill" about one hundred pages. Went to my d.a. for eleven but the doctor had called it for 11:30—waited around and bought a pop—knocked on her door and she smiled. I nuzzeleld into the chair with arms on it and almost had nothing to say. Asked why did I only see marna and no other girls—said I was probably afraid of being rejected and that both of us being sick we became dependent on each other to fill some of our needs. She shook her head. She had a phone call as usual and i finished off the pop quick like. Then asked if i could have Rich come and she allowed him. Asked if I could consentrate and I said yes, asked if i could go to summer school and she said it was too early to commit herself.

`looked at a book by picasso, his etchings, woodcuts and linoleum, very messy stuff but charming.`

Left fairly happy and then went TO lunch—am having trouble with the ribbon. Ate and came back to sleep—was awakened by 1:30 and went to the library where i filed some books, looked at a book by picasso, his etchings, woodcuts and linoleum, very messy stuff but charming. Then came back and fell asleep again. Was wakened for supper and had chicken and a sweet potato and then went to watch the dr-patient baseball or rather softball game. It was a lot of fun and then everyone walked back to the dining room so I had a chicken liver sandwich and sat with bob and helen and bob discussed colour and said he would show me how to mix them. Got into a conversation with a new patient named max, asked if i had improved and said i had, then enoumerated how; do not feel inferior, have no guilt feelings, any paranoic feelings, am able to speak to people, feel a little more disciplined, much freer, less inhibitions— that seems to be enough. Came back to the low and forgot to get a sandwich for bob—met him and played some ping pong and then asked if he wanted to go visit cindy—he did and we went. We all went into the back yard and started kicking around a dead volleyball, then we got to playing ping pong with a volleyball and i beat cindy. Then we just lay on the grass and talked silly nothings and then it got darker. We went inside and got attacked by some old ladies.

we just
lay on the
grass and
talked silly
nothings
and then it
got darker.

Then it was time for night activities. A concert by one zelda Schein a pianist. Went to concert, made paper planes out of the program. The concert was ok—my mind kept wandering to pastoral scenes such as [*camp*] winsoki and kinoza lake [*summer vacation colony*] and long beach [*summer cottage*]. I also got to thinking about Rich and how life is a struggle on the outside. Came back with bob—he offered me a cigarette and it was the first one in a long time. Smoked only half of it, went lying on the grass with candy—she talked about her family and i watched the stars. Am glad that I'm going out tomorrow, hope it's not as hot as it was today, will read some summerhill and then tom sawyer i think goodnight. The doctor still has my diary and i have mixed feelings about her having it but i guess it is for the best—the better she knows me the sooner i can get better.

saterday

part of a dream—am in a bank buying general motors stock at 23 dollars a share come out and find aunt esther giving away wine if you contribute to ashtma, uncle jack gives me a drink.

saterday april 26, 1962

woke at around eight fifteen rushed to breakfast and was one of the last to get served—ate quickly with don't remember whom who is awfully nice to have breakfast he's so quiet. Came back, didn't make my bed thinking that it being saterday none would bother me—they did and i had to reshuffle some of the covers. Phoned rich but woke him up so hung up. Then went upstairs and read approximately 50 pages of Klee's "the painter's eye". Was engrossed but felt my attention was lapsing so came back downstairs. Phil hadn't shown up and I was a little disappointed.

Jerked off and relaxed for fifteen minutes listening to wqxr. Then realised it was time to see dad—the door to the opd was locked so i had to walk all the way around to the gate—saw jays car and they came to pick me up, dad and jay came in I showed them my new paintings which they liked forgot to say i had a quick lunch of frankfurters, and then left after putting on lotion to keep old sol away. They didn't want to go into the city, saying it was too much traffic so I settled on the Brooklyn Botanic Gardens and Museum.

Had a nice drive, didn't get nausious, saw the skyline of new york which is always exciting and then parked a block away from the museum. Stole a book, "the Pedalogical Notebooks" of Paul Klee (a shorter version, much of bobs book) and then looked at some watercoulours and prints—wasn't too impressed by any, then saw ryder's "sea voyage" and some of his cows, dekoonings "woman"and a big picture by rivers full of life and a satire on family life. Recognized a lot of the painters by their style and was kind of proud. Then the family moved to the cafeteria and I left them to go to the toilet and to phone Rich. Saw some nice primitive designs on my way, went to the toilet and then called. Talked about not much—he still doesn't have a job and needs bread, mentioned grace but not pat. Mentioned drugs of cource and then said i should call him back during the week and we would throw the bull. Can't come tomorrow because he has a rehearsal. Went back and had my malted—some jokes were told and then we went to the botanical gardens.

The day was hot and hanging over us, but the cherry blossoms were out and I wished I could really paint. Was not too excited but enjoyed them. Then came upon a rediculously dressed model posing in everything but au natural, then upon a field of dead daffodils. Then the oriental gardens. They were quite something, relaxed as though time had two thousand years after this afternoon and had nowhere in particular to go. Got back to the car and went to aunt mary's. Bought a cake for daddies birthday, he was 59 today, and sung happy birthday along with aunt mary and Debbie [*Mary's niece*]. Debbie didn't know i was in a hospital and still doesn't i look so good. We talked mostly about and around richard [*Mary's son, who died of muscular dystrophy at seventeen*]—everyone misses him. Then we went to get some groceries and i went to a store called the ink well. Found nickerson's book "How I turned $1,000 into $1,000,000"—tried to steal it and a ray bradbury collection but the lady was watching too close. Saw that she had canvasses and bought five small ones. Mentioned i was in a hurry and she asked why? I answered quite honestly "You're not going to believe me but I am a patient from a mental hospital on my day off." She responded I looked ok and didn't charge me tax and wished me good luck. So I didn't steal any of her books on the way out. Dropped aunt mary off at dotties [*her sister*] and then came back. Signed in and ran to the dining room, the gates were closed but I managed to get through and had the last steak.

```
Stole a
book, "the
Pedalogical
Notebooks"
of Paul Klee...
then looked
at some
watercoulours
and prints—
wasn't too
impressed
by any...
```

Forgot to mention that we continued our argument about my having friends—the parents still trying to choose my friends for me and telling me to break relations with my friends. Asking leading questions etc. I told them to shut up.

Ate dinner with susan and some others, then came back to the low. Read the notes that lea and harold and david [*cousins*] wrote in the record they bought me, a mozart and aunt esther and uncle jack's record also. Went to visit cindy with my box of marshmellows, matches, and a hanger for roasting them. Couldn't find cindy so stopped in on phyllis—asked her if she wanted any and she said she never had any—susan said she wanted one. We talked and then I heard an aid walking by—I hid in the corner and phyllis started grinning. Mrs. Gordon came in and didn't see me and they burst out laughing—then she saw me and said i'd have to leave—meanwhile i stayed. Then I finally convinced phyllis she should have a marshmellow—I started one on fire and the aid said i'm not only in a girls room but I'm also starting fires.

Went out in back and saw jasmine looking at a still rabbit. Came in and knocked on marge's door—she said come in and I did. She was playing her recorder and i voiced how i would like to learn the piano—she said it took a long time to get any gratification from a piano. We talked mostly about reality and having childhood fantasies. She said her mother told her that she saw a scribbling in the subway saying "Mayor Wagner is a lesbian"—we both cracked up and went scurrying for some more conversation. I saw she had "franny and zooey" and remarked that it was a good book n'est ce pas—she related how one year she came home from smith [college] like zooey did (or was it franny)—then we talked about her friend whom I walked to the gate last week. I mentioned how it showed I was gaining courage to introduce myself and care for a girl and she said sandy had mentioned it in her letter. I asked where had she met her, sandy only being in high school—she said they both went to Buck's Rock work camp. I mentioned of cource joey miller and then sarah paul—she knew them but not ginny roth. We talked some more and the bell for activity rang and pretty soon a nurse came in so I left. Went to the dance but wasn't interested, so came back and put on one of my mozart records in donnie rudniks room and started reading really reading nickelson's book. Did that for a while and then came up for fresh air. And galen told me that a billy goldstein had called could i call him back in queens. I did and billy wants to come tomorrow. Told him to come through the gate or pose as rich cohen. Talked awhile and then cut the conversation short like the doctor told me.

The day was hot and hanging over us, but the cherry blossoms were out and I wished I could really paint.

Went back and did some more reading and listening and then it was time for drugs. And then john wanted to go to sleep so i came in here wanting to paint but saying the diary comes first. And started writing. Forgot to say that I enjoyed the day and even jay since i am expecting less and less of him and so enjoy him for what he is. When I was talking to rich i said my mother and father and big brother were here—he said you mean little brother and I laughed. Right now will paint a picture.

Sunday april 27, 1962

last dream was about a story that paul wrote and was reading, about killing people.

so i slept till eleven or twelve oclock daylight savings time. Woke and had a grapefruit for breakfast. Read two articles on henry miller which told me nothing. Started reading summerhill again and waited for al and bill. Waited till two thirty when bill showed up. Took him to see my pictures and he made no comment. Talked about his plans for the summer—he will go to california for a month and then has a job as a councelor for city children. He is working hard on some papers and has only three more weeks of school. I mentioned that I wanted to go to summer school and had asked my doctor but she wouldn't commit herself. Played him some ping pong and watched his body move.

listening to henry miller on the phonograph and hearing another man say that man is lonely, I recognized the shadow of myself seeking and reeking from aloneness.

I have gained so much weight that I look fat next to him—I really should do exercises. Walked him to the gate and then came back. Watched the program on picasso and it was fairly good. Went to see the picasso exhibits around town and will probably do that next saterday. The museum is also having an exhibit in the near future. Went to dinner and had scrambled eggs and bacon and macaroni and shells. Ate with bob. Then came back and went upstairs to listen to some of the new patients (jim) jazz records. He left for a walk after a while so i left and went to visit cindy, but stopped and talked with laura and jill greenberg—they asked me if i loved marna and said i once had but that now the relationship was sick. They asked me if I would marry her and I said no. Talked gossip about what girls i liked and said cindy, marge and amy—also pat as a big sister. and of course helen, louise and phyllis. Then left and visited cindy, marge and company, but marge was getting nervous that an aid would come so i left. Played some piano and then went to the movie. It was "Rhapsody" about liz taylor loving a violinist who is in love with only his violin. Another woman comes in—she tried to kill herself and is nursed back by a young neighbor pianist. She marries him, he turns into a lush and then to prove to the violinist that she is good she brings the pianist back to zurich and makes him practice. A moment before his first concert she tells him that she will leave with the violinist and he must be able to perform by himself. He does and she says no to the violinist they embrace and the end. The style was very static, very limited use of colour and scenery. Not much.

Forgot to say i painted a picture—no, two before the movie. One was the finishing of a cherry tree in rememberance of yesterday and the other was an abstract, a phallus type of yellow in the center rising with red and blue baroque inter twinings on either side. It gets nicer everytime i look at it. Then I wrote a poem to sam ware because tomorrow he leaves. He was the first friend i met here and his kind treatment of me helped a lot. His loaning me oils was very generous of him PLUS the many canvasses. I'll miss him but he is better and deserves to go back to living again. Someday soon maybe I'll be saying my adieus and that day shall be a grand and happy one. Good night.

> monday one
> watching people playing ping pong and it is really rediculous, right
> now am having two people arguing in my head
> he sleeps like a sickness ready to storm and enfold
> an evolving creature who walks, talks, and dances but now is dreaming dreams and dreams

A. S. Neill page 297 "how can happiness be bestowed? My own answer is: Abolish authority. Let the child be himself. Don't push him around. Don't lecture him. Don't elevate him. Don't force him to do anything. It may not be your answer. But if you reject my answer it is incumbent on you to find a better one."

listening to henry miller on the phonograph and hearing another man say that man is lonely, I recognized the shadow of myself seeking and reeking from aloneness. And every so often i remember that call it what ever you may but I am in a mad house. Cheerful, no?

Monday April 30, 1962

Woke early—had a full breakfast of wheatcakes two cereals and a cup of tea. Came back and read some of Summerhill, am almost finished and it has been a great book bringing forth a lot of my inhibitions and small fears which still fright me. Read till near ten when i went to o.t. I can't wait for farming and o.t. painted two pieces of furniture with sam and today was his final day here. I wanted to smother him in kisses and give him some good advise—instead we just joked as if life were going on forever which it probably will do.

Ate lunch right then and it was delisious, veal parmigian and other stuff. Came back to the low and browsed through the newspaper and the book review section, no—brought that to breakfast. At one point I had to go to volleyball and did. Played some ping pong first with a shmuck named peter robbins and then later with tim james and almost won the game against tim. Felt like I was playing chess. Talked with mrs lewis and told her how i was getting better. Told her that we both came here together only she was getting paid and i was paying. Then i went to see my loving doctor. Waited five minutes, enough time to either get anxious or compose myself—I did the latter. Talked about: if i was getting better, then said, but I don't have to even ask that question i know the answer and the doctor shook her head in approval. Then i told her about the argument that was going on in my head this morning between the two sides and i had no part of it. She asked me to associate and I said maybe my parents were arguing and I was trying not to take sides. Or maybe it was between god and me, then I said those associations are probably intellectualizations. Then i said i used to gulp my food down and associated jay's always waiting for me to finish my meals and then eating what i had left over, so now I don't have to eat fast. She returned my diary and asked for a comment knowing that i was silly to ask for one but she said it was good and that i should continue it—it would

painted two pieces of furniture with sam and today was his final day here. I wanted to smother him in kisses and give him some good advise— instead we just joked as if life were going on forever which it probably will do.

help her. In fact you'll be reading this too some day so hello dr esther plaut. I wonder if now i will block out certain things that i don't want you to know about, sub conscienouly or conscienously. well I wonder. Then i asked when will she let me know how long i'll be here and she said it is still too early.

Then as if by magic there was something else up her sleeve— she told me that tomorrow morning i have my initial conference. Will tell you about that after i have it. then told her that I stole a book on saterday and she asked me why and i said that i wanted it and didn't have any money and knew that the folks wouldn't let me have extra money so i copped it. She asked me why I told her and i said i guess i want to be punished, or scolded. Then i said i didn't see the difference between stealing the book or taking money from the folks. But i really do i think. She got me to say that i would return it or pay for it, but i have time and many promises to keep before i sleep.

Then went to sight singing but we only had fifteen minutes of it because miss lopez had to go away somewhere. I was satisfied. Came back and spoke with sam—then he decided to go and say goodbye to cindy so i went with him. Found cindy and susan and talked some. Tim James was there and handed cindy an envelope sealed. She held my arm for a while and after he left she told me why. She gets very nervous when he is around because he loves her and he is after all in his forties. The envelope contained a sonnet and cindy had given him a note asking not to see her again. She felt

Bob came
in and was
upset as
usual—I could
hardly reach
him and
I felt
inadequate,
but guess he
will have to
solve his own
problems and
not me.

miserable so i talked chearily—lisa joined and cindy and sam left. Asked susan if she would want to take up french with me and she said yes. Forgot to say that cindy snuggled up to me and said she loved me, which came as rather a shock. Stayed till five to five and then went to have pastrami then came back and read an article by ben-gurion on buddism which was enlightening. I want to read the "dharma putra" again. Then went to poetry which was on coleridge. First tried to get cindy to come but she wouldn't—she goes to sleep early now and is depressed, but she wouldn't come. It was pretty boring and i came back to the low.

Hear the new patient mickey singing an aria. Then went into Mickey's room and listened to henry miller talking on the phonagraph—it was good to hear a man talk again. Then i came back and started typing up my poems and a letter to alan and muriel. Bob came in and was upset as usual—I could hardly reach him and I felt inadequate, but guess he will have to solve his own problems and not me. He left and then a little later marty came in. I guess he is lonesome for ware. Then I went and got some schitzophrenic juice grapefruit and pineapple and took two more aspirins. I don't know what I'm getting these headances from maybe my cold. They are decreasing—now to read summerhill. Happy may i.

tuesday may 1, 1962

just came back from my initial conference and it wasn't too bad—there were lots of people and i just talked and talked. Dr. Fogel would ask me questions about why i got sick and when. I associated that i went to the unveiling the week before for uncle hymie [*our father's brother*]. And i felt guilty that the same thing was going to happen to father and that i really didn't care which is of cource untrue if I didn't care i wouldn't feel so guilty. He asked me how soon i thought i was getting out and i said six months—he said that was a good guess. Asked me what I wanted to do when I grow up? Answered a movie director. Asked what i wanted to do when i got out—I said get a good education at berkeley, and my second choice was queens. Told me i had a rather traumatic life which was encouraging because i thought i was just overdramatizing. Said was just getting over my operation now which is the truth and that don't feel guilty about things anymore. Nobody else said anything, and said i'm glad i'm not paranoid anymore all those people listening to me.

> Asked me what I wanted to do when I grow up? Answered a movie director. Asked what i wanted to do when i got out—I said get a good education at berkeley, and my second choice was queens.

Dr. Plaut waited for me and then took me into the conference room where everyone was waiting: mr. arms, mrs stevens, mrs. schwartz, the head nurse and then mr. trucks came and dr. fogel. He asked all the questions. I was not nervous or shy and was quite proud that i was quick on the response and answered all the questions that were asked. I feel quite free now and know that i am getting better and am fairly close to really learning how to use some of my talents. I am enjoying more things now and interested in things generally.

Came back and read the paper and a comic book to relieve some of the tension. Went to lunch and met Phyllis and talked about my initial conference and even telling her that i had my testicle removed [*at the age of 13*] as if it were an appendix. I am not ashamed anymore and intellectually know that it just happened and was not a punishment or anything. Dr. Fogel said two nice things. One—why would god bother to punish me, and 2) our fantasies (including mine, he said) are not that strong that they act themselves out.

Had a delisous lunch of steak and potatoes and lettuce and tomato. Came back and went to get a haircut with mr. Olds. I tried very hard to talk to him and got him to say that he wants a car, but that was all. After my haircut went to the library, maybe next time i can go by myself. Took out three books on real estate one on Bosch and one by Lawrence about his travels in Italy. It was drissling a little when we came back. Mr. Olds wanted to stop and buy garters, and i giggled for some reason. Came back and read some and then changed to sneakers for dance therapy and went. Got tired at times and stopped. For some of the music i started galloped hitting my rear as i galloped and the rest of the people stood around and clapped, so now i have regained my sponteneity.

For some of the music i started galloped hitting my rear as i galloped and the rest of the people stood around and clapped, so now i have regained my sponteneity.

Forgot to say that dr. aczel was at the confeence probably forgot because i was worried about how i did on the tests. Came back and started reading "How to make money Speculating in Real Estate"—read about 40 pages when I was called for the new patients meeting. Was a little set back that my doctor still thinks i need it. Wasted an almost hour listening to mr. Arms. Then he went over my program. I then went to donnies room and listened again to Henry Miller. He is just another guy only he happened to have a passion named writing. He has a curious phrase that he uses all the time—"don't you know." Then went to supper, had a hamburger and some coliflower, ate with marty and roz and tom—they were joking about making it with a pussy kat and i volunteered that i once tried to make it with a dog, aunt evelyns boxer, who still knows and likes me. Everytime i come i am greated by doxie giving me a big smack kiss and wanting to go for a walk.

Came back and read some more, trying to control a headache— I had earlier taken two aspirins and now asked for two more. Went to choral club but the piano was locked and I didn't want to sit through that so I returned and read some more. Then floated out and talked with bob and maryse. And then bob alone—he said i was

Today was may day and i saw no parade or maypole. next year where will i be—in california? israel? a mental hospital?

a good guy and I immediately switched the subject but was gleeming from proudness. Asked him what boswell had to say and he gave me some quote—"every man who writes writes for money or else is a fool"—something like that. I said I must be a fool. But he said that boswell remembered conversations and things and i felt jealous. I know I'm not doing too good a job on this but i think i am improving and getting less mechanistic and more to what is really happening.

Then went out to the lobby and passed the time talking small talk. Then went to playreading and read a funny play by shaw and then a boring one. Then came back and started writing. Forgot to mention what happened last night before i went to sleep. Marty had come in and was reading jimanez and then his own poems in spanish and english.

Today was may day and i saw no parade or maypole. next year where will i be—in california? israel? a mental hospital? good night

Wednesday may 2, 1962

It is early being only about eight thirty but i feel that I will feel better if i write now and then have time to read or maybe talk or listen to some music.

Refused to get up again today—finally did—came back and was told that my sheets were changed (just came back from watching a detective program and Sam G broke a window, well now some real life action something that every american waits for but somehow i'm not too interested, only that this may mean sam's being transferred to some other hospital. I've come to believe in hillside and that it will help all those who help themselves or at least try).

Went back to bed and had to be coaxed back to life, but i really think that i enjoy when everyone tries to wake me up—it makes me think people are concerned enough of this foolishness—tomorrow i'll get up. Made the bed and cleaned up. Took Klee's "pedagogical Sketchbook" and went to o.t. But didn't have to work—instead Mrs. Stevens planned out the farm, so I read some and then just sat there bored. Came back to the low and went into Donnie Rudnik's room—heard the last side of the miller album and realized that he's just another man who happened to write with his little set of stories and jokes and that someday when all the fanfare is over i will have to live out my life like anyone and/or everyone else. Then read Dwight Macdonald's column on movies and was entertained and then came back and painted two pictures. One a klee-type humorous one with four figures alternating male and female red and yellow against blue, brown and green. I also put a blue frame around the picture—it is very beautiful looking and the first picture that i have done. Then I did an abstract in the watercolouring book that marna gave me. It is whole or integrated i think. Then finished summerhill—satisfied an then went to my D.A. I didn't know which book to take, Klee or the real estate one, took the real estate so i wouldn't feel guilty having stolen the klee. Doctor asked me what i was reading and I told her and then

Went back to bed and had to be coaxed back to life, but i really think that i enjoy when everyone tries to wake me up—it makes me think people are concerned...

explained myself saying the idea interested me more than monopoly or bridge—she asked me what i would do if I were rich i said loaf, write, paint and travel. She didn't say anything but i think she had a smile. Asked her what happened at the initial conf, after i left and she said they talked about putting direction into my life and becoming disciplined—all the things that I had just told her. I had said that I finished Summerhill and felt good having read it because now i wouldn't fear as much having kids. I laughed and said it was a little early speaking about kids but that I wanted to have foresight now and live a somewhat planned life. So it seems that my aims and the doctors'are approximately the same, which is healthy.

> I laughed and said it was a little early speaking about kids but that I wanted to have foresight now and live a somewhat planned life.

Then she said what would i think of having a foster home. For three minutes i was speechless, then I said it was what i have always asked for but how would my parents take it, and i guess i still feel dependent on them and need them. She said alright—I didn't have to decide now, it was something that we could talk over some other time. Then she said the social worker Mrs. Reardon would be seeing my brother and father, and i said good—jay is sicker than me. I said i thought i had done well at the conference and felt satisfied—she shook her head. Then i started talking about being alone and my opinion that all men are ultimately alone. Then she sprang another surprise—how would i like group therapy—I got scared and said at this time i would prefer da's. But then i said maybe i'll realize that other people have problems and it will make me less lonely. Also there would be another doctor, so that maybe it was something that I could look forward to. Then I told her that I wanted out of the new patients group and she said alright.

I then went to the library and they were choosing records that we would buy this month. I reeled off names—bartok, L'histoire du soldat by stravinski, mjq, then we discussed discussing books and i suggested to kill a mockingbird and then i thought to myself why don't we have here at the hospital a "Great Books Club"—I'd have to take that up with Mrs. Levine in charge of volunteers so i will. Forgot to say that when I came back from lunch i stopped into the library and looked at the klee book. After i started talking to a woman named eva and she said she liked me and that she felt like my mother and maybe she would adopt me after i told her what dr. plaut said.

I notice now that i have a compulsion to tell people what happens at my d.a.'s. I guess i am not satisfied with dr. plauts love and i want love and affection (how are they different) from everyone else. Then went to dinner at 4:30 and had delishous chinese meal called pepper steak, had two of them. Came back and went up to bob's room after asking him if i could look at the klee book. Started to but wasn't interested—played tim james about five games of ping PONG AND LOST ALL OF THEM NATURALLY. did not mean for all that to be in capitals—the machine went bad again. Then started going to current events but said if the library was open i was going there. So i read the current atlantic about money. Then i went upstairs to the dance but wanted to see cindy. Talked for a while to Phyllis again about my d.a. and that she is going home saterday for the first time in nine and half months—she is very excited. Then met marge and cookie—they walked back to low 2 with me but cindy was sleeping. So we walked to the vending machines and stood around laughing till about 8:20 and then i showed them my picture and gave marge why bat a ball thing. They liked the picture very much but they had to go so I came back to the ward and started typing.

thursday

just as i was falling asleep my mind would associate with the talk going on. Things were very clear just lit a candle and uttered a prayer, if i were a catholic i would light candles all the time. My prayer is to get better quicker

ten o'clock

finally woke after some nagging—went to breakfast. Read the times and came back—was nagged about the room so I cleaned it up. Started reading again the real estate book which is good reading and takes the place of fantasying. I am trying not to hypnotize myself by the candle and now i remember for some reason beth furman's room in san francisco. She was fat and i was hard up but still i was afraid—will i always be afraid of women's bodies? I wasn't with marna. Forgot to call tonight. Went to o.t. and read some more during break also. Stayed for lunch which was what? stayed and talked with? maybe susan and some others but don't remember who or what. Came back and called up mom and felt funny because of the doctor's telling me about foster parents i felt already as if she weren't my parent—something which i have wanted to feel for a long time.

just lit a candle and uttered a prayer, if i were a catholic i would light candles all the time. My prayer is to get better quicker

Had lunch with carl, it was beef stew and noodles. Talked about the dramatics which is boring. Then went to the government meeting which also was boring. After had a game of ping pong with howie and almost won. Then started reading the real estate book again. Stopped at 3 and went to the library but it was closed so i went looking for mrs. Safter who would take care of the great books but she railroaded me to mr. roberts so i went to see him. He will take care of a letter and who knows? I would be very happy if one were started especially if it were done because of my asking. Went to the library and finished reading Wescott's appreciation of Katherine Anne Porter and thought delishously of the books Book of the month club is sending—"Ship of Fools" and the compleat Short Stories of Earnest Hemingway. Susan came in and asked if I wanted to practice french and i did so came and went to the back but she wasn't there so rounded her up but didn't really want to read french, so she got out a science book which she will let me use tomorrow. I feel as though my mind is not rotting but being partially occupied. then went to supper which was liver and hash brown potatoes—ate with marty and roz. Marty put me down for saying that Kafka was neurotic, but he was! Then we talked about the inability to communicate. My typeing is really bad—something else for me to improve. Then sat with cindy, marge and susan—joked and coming back yelled jibberish to cindy and was quite histerical laughing and falling out. Then went to science class. But got goofy and started falling asleep. My doctor has switched the thorazine time giving it to me in the afternoon instead of late at night. I was feeling very tired all afternoon and finally realized what it was from. So i excused myself and came back and slept. Had a series of almost nightmares. In one of the dreams i was slapping father. Woke at nine thirty and drank some juice and played three hands of whist. I can not understand how people, intelligent and sensitive, can play all day. Now I'll read tom sawyer and some real estate.

I can not understand how people, intelligent and sensi-tive, can play all day. Now I'll read tom sawyer and some real estate.

Friday may 4, 1962

I am writing this on saterday since there was a ten thirty curfew last night and i watched twighlight zone. Woke up—had a full breakfast and read some tom sawyer, then went with everyone else for the picnic. Walked to the busstop and then went into the candy store, stole two books, one a collection of jewish biographies and the other the best short stories of 1961. Went to alley pond park and started to pitch. They choozed up teams and i was to pitch. I thought for awhile that i was back in camp. Struck out two or three batters but got slaughtered, the sides were quite uneven. then we walked to the campfire site and had hamburgers and franfurters for lunch. Afterwards we had a folk sing and then some picnic games. then we came back. They needed someone to clean up the grills and i volunteered after bob did. Came back by car (saved fifteen cents) and washed up the grills. Then went to work in the library. At three i went to the UN group although I was exhausted. The leader was talking about her trip to Washington and i told the group of the brooklyn botanic gardens. Then they talked about disarmament and I made a little speech about how the u.s. has surrounded the ussr with bases. Afterward we got to talking with the leader, forget her name, and she said she painted some and then asked me if i graduated from college—I said how come she asked and she said because i had so much knowledge.

Forgot to say that during the session i was reading a thesis that some guy wrote about when he was working as the library leader here at hillside. It was very interesting and made me more aware that i am being watched for how i socialize and how i respond to frustrating expeiences, and work tasks. Then i asked her if she would like to see my paintings and brought her back to the low. She liked them very much and was surprised by the number of styles that i have used. Then i showed her the two poems that I have written since I've been here, one to cindy and the other to sam—she wanted copies of both. I was almost in a fevered frenzy at such appreciation.

Went to dinner and don't remember anything that happened. Came back and smoozed around, first with cindy and the girls and then played ping pong for a solid half hour. Went to evening activity after i staffed the library for a half an hour. Read some F. L. Wright. The evening activity was charades so i was in a fix whether or not to volunteer but then i remembered how many times i have made a fool of myself in public and didn't want to now. In a while i will be able to approach public activity without that fear. Afer a while came down to make a few phone calls. Talked to dad and mother and felt like a traitor when I was talking to mommy because of the parent bit. She told time and again how much she loved me and how i was improving and i felt all hot and bothered. Then called sue—got no answer and tried several times after. Finally got her and had a long conversation about my treatment here and i was very positive about the therapy program. I told her that I did not want to become psychotic again, and that i wanted to be productive and claimed that i had made some beautiful pictures in high school and i asked her but how often did i do anything. And that now i am most of the time happy whereas before it was usually depression. Came back to the low in time to watch the twighlight zone. It was about a ventriloquist and his dummy and how they slowly switch places. It was very frightening but only a piece of fiction. Had a hard time falling asleep, probably from a number of reasons. The conversation with mother and sue and the fact that i didn't unwind by writing. Finally went to sleep per my usual method.

The evening activity was charades so i was in a fix whether or not to volunteer but then i remembered how many times i have made a fool of myself in public and didn't want to now.

Saterday may 5, 1962

went to breakfast had three grapefruits. Came back and slept till lunch. Al didn't show up for the how many times since he said he would come and i was angry and lonely. Had lunch with Phyllis, bob and helen, just like old times. Afterwards played a game of scrabble with phyllis and lost and felt very bad about the game even though i had a high score of 235. Marge brought me the whole cource in speedwrighting and that is what I'm going to do now. See you later tonight.

Did two and half lessons in speedwrighting and enjoyed them. It will be of great value when i go back to school taking notes. Also played a little piano. Then watched the ceremonies leading up to the kentucky derby but fled when informed that it was five thirty. Ate spaghetti with tim james and then walked back with ned laifer slow at his pace. Went to low two conference room after a phone call from sue. She will come tomorrow and last weekend she went to green camp (from cooper union) and made a kite but it is too big to bring in. This is her last week of school and then she'll go to berkeley for the summer. Bill Goldstein is also going to California and pretty soon when i am well i will be going there too. Thought over again the foster parent idea and liked it. Phyllis was listening to some opera and then helen and bob came in, then bob came back with a carvel sundae which he gave to me. As soon as helen leaves he will start giving me lessons again but i don't want helen to leave. But as dr fogel said that my fantasies aren't that strong, my wishing her to stay and get better aren't going to make her stay. Then came back with ed and listened to Mozart piano concertos. I finished reading tom sawyer which was a lot of fun. It was strange that i should read both summerhill and twain at the same time. I am glad however that i am growed up and all the time getting older. Also wiser and happier. The weather was grand today and sitting outside in the back with the trees and the visitors was fun. There is a new crop of tulips up the daffodils are dead and soon

It was strange that i should read both summerhill and twain at the same time. I am glad however that i am growed up and all the time getting older.

summer will sweep sizzling in. I hope i am off thorazine by then so i can go swimming.

I surprise myself by the little thinking that i do. Most of my thinking has always taken place verbally unless its all unc/subconscienous—life is not so boring any more now that i am learning to amuse myself. I wish i could write stories but i fear that i have nothing to write about so i put down poems and scribble off paintings. By next week i hope to have some masonite so that i can enlarge my paintings. tomorrow will be spent with the family including jay and i hope it is nice and that i don't get upset. Of cource i will take along aspirin.

There is a
new crop of
tulips up the
daffodils are
dead and soon
summer will
sweep siz-
zling in. I
hope i am off
thorazine by
then so i can
go swimming.

sunday may 6, 1962

had a full and fun day but will start at the beginning for narrations sake. Woke at nine, but woke much earlier and had the ambition to get up and read but didn't . Had a petit dejeuner and then waited for sue and deb. They came later, around ten and by that time i had diagnosed one case of stiff neck. Took some aspirin to releave some of the pain but it was bad. Took them to low two and they met mrs. Stevens and we talked a little about hypnotism and offered some of my experiences with elise this summer and how i was afraid to go too far. Then we went up to see amy who happens to be a friend of deb's. We gossiped and then sue and i sat down to talk.

had a full
and fun day
but will
start at the
beginning for
narrations
sake.

We talked about her trying to get along with her parents and then she tried to remind me how talented i was with words and people, how i made her feel like a person in high school and i agreed and said that more and more i was feeling human and likeable. She had a new bag beautiful, it must be mexican or something she got it at the brooklyn museum. Before we started talking it was eleven so i walked her to the gate. Deb was going to stay and go on to the museum with the family. But I couldn't stop at the gate so i walked her to the bus stop. By the time we came back i heard a voice calling—it was jay and then from nowhere marna came masquerading as liz taylor or again katherine hepburn.

So i came back to the low to check out and they saw my pictures saying nothing but leaving three new canvasses (sue said my figures were good—so there). We left and I got car sick so we stopped and i had a coke. then we couldn't decide if we should go to the museum or the parc—we finally concurred that the parc would do since the museum wouldn't open till one. We had a nice picnic lunch near a lake and watched all the boaters boating. Then we went to the museum and i wanted to go through the whitney and save some money but they wouldn't hear of such a thing. Deb thought the plan most good. So we went to the third floor first and saw the picasso exhibit and it was wonderful. His lines were so clean and clear and definite. And his subjects were varied but repeating. Saw mostly drawings from his blue period.

Then went to the movies and they had nine magnificent shorts (I am including the museum memo so that I needn't repeat myself.) The movies were all in polish but so well done visually that one understood all the time what was happening. In contrast to "the Court Marshall of billy mitchell" which we saw this evening which could have been a radio broadcast for all the camera added to it.

Then deb and i went to the whitney but they had a bad show—geometrical abstractionists. they looked mostly like what a crossword puzzle fan would do if he painted. Came back and saw the second floor. They had lots of picasso's sketches for "Guernica" and it was most enlightening. Also saw some pollack and lots of klee paintings—they were a disappointment.

Left deb off but first walked to radio city and was fascinated by the water designs left on the pavement by the short rain. There were horses and just lots of shapes. Came back not saying very much—feeling very guilty about wanting foster parents and that i was no longer part of them. They harranged me about museam visiting and a few incidentles but told me that the social worker said i might only stay six months if i kept up at the pace that i did. Came back and showed helen and bob my newest paintings and then went to the dull movie. Came back and started talking to bob about the film and what i did today and then about dreams. He said that his dreams were reality and living a nightmare—I agreed but said that the happier he got the closer his dreams would come to reality. He said that there were only two things that were worth living for—love and imagination. He then said that friendship was a form of love. I agreed and thought that our relationship was a great and good one. Then simpson chased him out and said everyone to bed—that means me too.

I feel bugged down and hung up for a pussy
willow tree to piss cucumbers pickled on me

The movies were all in polish but so well done visually that one understood all the time what was happening. In contrast to "the Court Marshall of billy mitchell" which we saw this evening which could have been a radio broadcast for all the camera added to it.

foggin the sea in summer
when sands and time seem to simmer and shift
flowing in waves like the crakling calming blue pacific
that i now remember with regret that i ever
returned to madness and grey oceans of people waiting
for their little plot of green wild weeds overgrown
*

why must i always look for books
as if their crooked authors could tell me anything
I can only hear what i understand and that fluctuates
and now that spring is stealing green from seeds and things
I only have to watch and remember when i blink my eyes
what it was
that i was watching wretching and welcoming to hello and
introduce
myself to these new guests who stay until seasons surrender
unto
one another and finally fell the little patches of greensome in
fall

monday may 7, already nearer to ten

feel absolutely lousy. feel like an old man and ache and feel my stomach as if it were grinding itself out of existence. My neck still hurts even after them giving me a drug but o well tomorrow is another day and there will be many more. No suicides from this author. Refused to even get up this morning so i missed breakfast and rationalized that i could lose some weight. Had a variety of dreams as usual and last night was one of the first in a long time that i fell asleep without jerking off pardin the language. Went to o.t. thinking we were going to farm—the seeds didn't arrive yet so we had to paint furniture again. Went out for a break and mickey told me there was a package for me in the mail room. I thought it would be the book of the month club but it wasn't—it was a package sent by aunt marcia and was very strangely shaped—I couldn't figure out what it was. Came back to the low and opened it—it was two sketch pads and a box of pastels and charcols, very nice and as usual aunt marcia was nice. I have always liked her and respected her even with all the animosity on mothers part to her—I still remember feeling guilty when the phone rang on that rosh hashanna night and it was to announce that uncle izzy [*marcia's husband; our mother's brother*] was dead, and i thought that god was punishing the family for my wrongdoings—that was when i still thought i was a prophet or shortly after.

Listened to some fm mozart and started reading chloe marr again by milne—it is a very funny book rediculing the social life of middle upper england—a sort of spoof on evelyn waugh type spoofs. Went to lunch but there was an intolerably long line because they are messing around with the time schedual—I was told it will be back to normal tomorrow. So I came back and wrote the two poems on the page previous. Then went to lunch and had lilly garber, she telling me all about hitler and his egomania and manic and paranoic states. All from her reading Shirer's book which she said was weak, him being more of a gossiper or frustrated diplomat than historian (sic). I said that if a book gets on the best

```
feel
absolutely
lousy…but o
well tomorrow
is another
day and there
will be many
more. No
suicides from
this author.
```

seller list then i automatically assume that there is something weak about the book. (But i would have to omit to kill a mockingbird, franny and zooey, and i haven't read ship of fools yet). Then talked with susan and by the time i came back it was time to go to volleyball.

Went reluctantly and waited, playing rather poorly until they called me to the medical clinic for my neck. Then I came back and tried to read until it was time for sight singing. Started a book in Mr. Hill's room by hindemith on music theory and if i have any guts i will continue to read it. Then went to sight singing and surprised myself that i could follow so well and actually could spot the notes. Came back and played some ping pong until it was time for supper. Again we had to wait and there was an even bigger line this time but i managed to get in front (cheating again so i am not an existentialist saying what i do is universally good, no i try to be expediante and i am a sinner but there are times when it is almost a matter of survival and i do survive). I had become very anxious, my stomach ready to eat and there being no food. Finally got my stuffed cabbage and sat down with cindy and marge. They were making funny poems but i hadn't the stamina to join them. Came back to the low and played some ping pong with donnie. I think he is getting better he speaks more or maybe i am just becoming friends and there fore he trusts me so can speak more—again i am trying to be doctor only it is not as much fun as the games of doctor i used to play with cousin janice.

then went searching for the poetry group but it seemed that they weren't meeting tonight. Again heard the rumor that they (the they) are going to change around the doctors and the wards and i want my doctor.

Then played tennis for the second time, this time with mr. hill. Was doing very well when my hands started itching so i decided to call it quits. Then went to the library and looked at a big book on Joyce by Ellman. Skimmed it which surprised me—I am learning how to read faster. Came back to the low in time for some games

> I am not an existentialist saying what i do is universally good, no i try to be expediante and i am a sinner but there are times when it is almost a matter of survival and i do survive.

and riddles that mr. arms had designed—have to go to toilet be back—am back.

Had some fun then went to talk to bob—when i left i said i felt like it was a b..a. he said yeah—a bob appointment. I told that if we moved to cottage d I wished he was my roomate and he said yeah. I got to talking about california and he said by the way i described it i must have been pretty depressed yes i was yes i was. Made up my mind to get up by seven tomorrow morning and eat and then come back so i can watch educational t.v. a program from columbia. We'll see if i can get up. Maryse was in here looking at my paintings and poetry and i felt like i had a big sister. She is very beautiful but why is she alone. And why do i always want to know if people are married why my fixation—naturally i am afraid of getting married and becoming like dad. I wonder if there will be just one woman in my life. Let's see if i can write another poem.

> where does the green come from that decorates those trees
> which sit and stand upon that queens carpet green?
> and why do flying things nest there in?
> and me stay inside these walls of stone
> do leaves get cold? or catch a cold
> when rain rains and washes beyond each branch
> and when did these new leaves have time to make friends with
> the wind?
> *
> on a grey day what's there to do but
> sleep sleep or creep around exploring attics of my
> mind
> and keep the rind of yesterday doings carefully
> kept and wept for knowing now what wasn't known then
> when eveything was as it was
> so in summary these days have some value
> they give us rest to wrestle with those unkept things
> which bring disasterloos if not watched and bewhitched.

tuesday may 8, 1962 nine oclock

had a very relaxful day. with one funny. Refused to wake up again—got pulled out of bed after several dreams—still haven't got enough discipline to either wake up or write down my dreams but time, everything takes time. Had a bridge lesson till half past 11, went to lunch—forget what we had or whom i ate with. Came back and went to sleep. It was a very gooslip grey day and i enjoy sleeping. I remember how snobby i use to be when sid burick would sleep all day or even jay and how i thought i would never get like that. Well I've gotten.

Got woken at three—had nothing to do so i started doing speedwriting—was much slower than i thought i would be. Also read a story by will Sayroyan—very beautiful and then wasted some time playing ping pong. then came back and glanced through another real estate book and then the how to read faster book. It seems that today was a day of self improvement. Ran to dinner since it was close to five thirty. Ate by myself a horrible kind of stringy steak. Came back and was bored so i put on a tie to cheer me up and went to low two. Went looking for marge and cindy (really don't know which one i was really looking for, for discipline sake i will describe them—cindy a beautiful dusty brown haired girl. Very light on her feet—looks most of the time as if she were dancing—small breasts pointed wears a mouthbite. Blue eyes, about five six. Writes poetry, is very gentle, sings instead of talks, sometimes whispers, has had a year at brooklyn college, draws very well and writes good poetry. Naïve (see poem: little bird of beauty. marge, petit girl usual music and art [*high school*] complexion dark, wears hanging earrings, long stringley hair, has a slight mustashe, rather pretty looking intellectual spent a year at smith college. Very quick, likes to laugh. Finally they showed up—cindy was balancing a basket on her head and then marge and i tried both successfully.

Went to marge's room, laughed some, hit the bat and ball and then got thrown out by a nurse. Went to the day room and they compiled a funny poem that is enclosed. Marge rewrote it in speed wrighting and I saw how useful it can become. Then i came back for my two poems, no 3 and they liked parts of them. Then we got to talking about the doctors and how free each of us felt with them. Marge remarked did i like a woman doctor i said yes and it was probably because most of my problems were with my mother—they both agreed and then i started to say i have always wanted to attend my mothers wedding but said instead i have always wanted to attend her funeral.

Went to marge's room, laughed some, hit the bat and ball and then got thrown out by a nurse.

We laughed for about five minutes straight—it was a very funny slip. Then it was time to come back. Playreading was cancelled as was chorus so i spent my time visiting with maryse and then bob. He was very sleepy as usual and so i left him to come type. Saw my notice of my orientation for creative therapy and and getting anxious. Have come around to sort of expecting foster parents or at least better relations with the ones i have. Now want to read chloe.

Wednesday

changing sheets day and the perfect day to realize that one is not only living but enjoying it too.

had k.p. this morning but refused to get up so i slept through breakfast again. Changed my sheets with out much argument and made my bed right then and there so i wouldn't have it hanging over me all day. Went to work group and we had farming—turned over earth—first everything was dry and then it was rich brown soil. Started picking up rocks too. When we went to put away our shovels al through his and broke a big window. He jokingly said why did you do that, neugeboren? miss johns asked why did i do it. I immediately answered that it was a axident and thought that i had to cover up for al but that i could take it—nice, no? Later she asked why i did and i said i didn't but wouldn't tell who did. She left it at that. Went to a late lunch but again there was a long line—sat down with phyllis helen and bob and for the first time i felt independent—I felt as if i was doing them a favor by sitting with them and that we could have a good time—not guilty about me being the little cute kid to ask all the questions.

Finally got my meal and sat next to pat. Lou came and sat down which pleased me but all three of us said nothing until pat craked— "what do you think of abortion"—that broke the ice and somehow we started talking. Went back and started reading again "How to make money speculating in real estate." Then told me i had to go to newspaper but there was none. Didn't go to volleyball because i wanted to read. Then the library opened up and i read there. Then we had a rather uneventful meeting but it was noted that practically all of the staff was leaving soon. I shone with thinking that that meant that I would become president. Having more responsibilities and perking up the library, fantasied writing nice letters to publishers and getting lots of free books. Staffed the library till supper time and heard one good mozart (just cleaned myself up for the first time in a long time—have to hurry past ten thirty). Went to late dinner, guzzled the food—fishcakes and had the pleasure of watching cindy eat. She has smorgasboard every-

changing
sheets day
and the per-
fect day to
realize that
one is not
only living
but enjoying
it too.

time she eats she goes from one left over tray to another—I once told them how i used to do that at the guggenheim and one day i picked a pastrami sandwich that had someones nails in it.

Then asked her what she did today and she said nothing in a very depressed way and i tried to cheer her up by telling her that a watched pot never boils and that she had to start somewhere even if it were anywhere and that after a while she would begin to get involved in things but that she mustn't watch herself so closely. She said that she enjoyed nothing and i tried to disprove her—then i asked her if she would like to come to the library and she said she didn't care, but that she never spoke with anyone like she did with me, and thanked me then. She signed out and came. I showed her the Steinberg book and she laughed but then her aid came and she told the aid that she signed out but we both giggled because she is on restrictions. The aid came back and so cindy finally—third time—she got an aid to stay with her. In between i wrote this poem:

```
In the first
act there was
a marvelous
tension pro-
duced by both
leading char-
acters—one
felt as if
they should
touch or
embrace but
they didn't.
```

> the love between us
> grows like ivy
> poisoned and itchy
> it goes up and down my skin-shell
> goosing me into pimples
> and all i know
> blows away before your asking heart

Finished the real estate book and then had a whole bunch of people come in. Marty and amy came in and started talking jibberich and I had to tell them to keep quiet. They left and came back—I started reading the carver book and then showed cindy the human comedy by sayroyan but she wasn't interested in anything. Then closed up shop and went to the aud for a play. Am enclosing the program. A few things about it. In the first act there was a marvelous tension produced by both leading characters—one felt as if they should touch or embrace but they didn't. Then i couldn't get over the idea that grown people were doing something just for fun. Bob related it to the family, saying that my parents probably never opened their eyes. I agreed and said that was why i needed foster parents. I said at one point that the play was just the horatio alger story and Dick Hayes said i was too far out—I didn't know whether to take that as a compliment or not. Some of the acting was good and parts of the play were too. It was a very good buildup till the last act where it bogged down in mediocrity as most browdway vehicles do. Afterwards amy and marty went to get their autographs but i couldn't do it with out laughing. Amy really is hip. Then bought ice cream for me and bob and loaned him a dollar for tomorrows bike trip. Talked about being a coward and i said i was a coward when i stole. Because i was refusing to commit myself. That if i had to pay money for books then i would have to read them and work to earn them but that this way i could come or go. Bob said it was very sick and i think i said not very. Our relationship amazes me in that it keeps on growing, plus for the first time i felt as if i really loved a girl again and we shall see i guess. Doctor comes back tomorrow and feel good. Feel as though i am independent and working out a lot of things. Pretty soon you should be reading some good poetry or recording the production of some nice art work.

Whom are you anyway you are just a part of me
how come you've shoocken awake
to break through dreams
for this?

thursday may 10

am very tired—took my thorazine early. Woke after breakfast but had time to read and will wake early tomorrow with a little effort. Started reading archy and mehitable and then went to farming. Planted and watered some corn seeds but was getting burnt so i returned to the low. Went to lunch and talked with a janet zelenko—told her my idea for solving the world problems. Start an international city which would be a refuge for peace lovers. Then when it was successful set up states all around the world. She liked it. Had a government meeting and then went bike riding. It wasn't as much fun as last time—we had to go up lots of hills but i feel in better shape. Stopped for a malted and stole two books. Saw the bay. Came back and couldn't eat, I was so itchy from sunburn. Went to take a shower and did—it was very relaxing and after i combed my hair. Went visiting and met sandra and talked with her. One of the girl's nurses remarked on how well i looked and i said i felt the same way. Met bob gold and he said i was much calmer than i was when i came in. Went to the adult lounge and watched a manic in action—noticed that he held his neck stiff the same way that marty did—is it a good observation or just coincidence? Came back and phoned up father—talked for a long time and then called bill goldstein. Then rushed in to see hiroshima mon amour—it was good. But the television medium and dubbing marred it. Was reminded of marna but not so much—am looking for new affairs. Sam ware is sleeping on the grounds after running away from home, and my first instinct is to give him a lecture to go home. I am fearful that something might happen to him and his life would be cut short. will write tomorrow morn.

friday may 11, 1962 i think

hurrah! I woke this morning in time to go to breakfast—came back and watched the last part of the columbia lectures—it was about the political parties in western europe, how most of the countries are dominated by either christian democrats or social democrats and their losing of power of the fascists. Then came back to sleep but mr. elder got on my ass and stripped my bed so i remade it.

Then read the times and started revising my diary for the doctor but didn't finish it by the time i had a d.a. Went there with nothing much on my mind except to discuss my homosexuality and if it were a thing of the past. I explained that i didn't want to have sex with any of my friends now and that now i have a good self image of my self and i feel like a man. Related how i stole the two books on thursday and I'll have to return them tomorrow. Got two passes, one with the folks tomorrow to see a movie and one with jay on sunday to go to the metropolitan and maybe to see jules and jim or last year at marienbad. Also told her of how i almost lecture sam ware this morning and told him that there was nothing in california. That everything is within.

Had a fish for lunch and some fried eggplant which wasn't very good. Came back and went to sleep. Then went to the library and did some tasks and then we had a bagel and lox party and they brought a group around on orientation and there was a new girl amongst them whom i had met on my way out from lunch. She was reading 100 modern poems so immediately i started conversing with her—she is very talkative and maybe a good prospect. Then went to UN group and got coney island of the mind from mrs silver. Came back and goofed for some time, then went back and had roast beef—ate with cindy and then marge came—it was very pleasant. Forgot—before dinner went to visit cindy, had a nice half hour.

Talked with lou at o.t. again about myself and talked at the dinner table about some of my adventures. Came back and started a painting—first got down to my underwear and felt quite free. The painting isn't very good but it is a start on figures. Then bob came in and we went to the library. I took out the book on primitive art and it was a gas—they have such great designs. Then decided to call home and tell them about the change in plans—they'll come tomorrow after schull. Then went back to the library and met laura there. She was reading an accountacy book but we started conversing. Just small talk. Then i went up to the auditorium where they were having a folk singing session—it was kinna boring. Came back to the low after calling bill not to come tomorrow afternoon. He may come in the morning just to say hello. Forgot to say that they took sam to creedmore—I hope they'll let him back in here but it seems fairly unlikely. Came back and bob got that glarey look in his eyes and started fake punching lee—then he went back to his room and gathered up his money and said he was leaving. There was nothing that i could say to him. I'll go to him now but first i want to unload a compliment. I was telling janet how i thought foster parents would be good because it would tell me that some people loved me. And she said that everyone here at the hospital loves me—I was rather pleased. Am getting what may be tension pain in my upper chest but feel very relaxed who knows goodnight.

Came back and started a painting— first got down to my underwear and felt quite free.

Saterday may 12, 1962

woke up with a stiff neck again, terrible hurting—think i have cancer or something (what is something?)—go to breakfast and rush back so i can see sunrise semester. A negro is talking about american black men. Then they have a reading skill program and i start snoozing so return to the room and wake after several attempts at sleep and quite a few dreams by eleven. Complain and get to see the rounds doctor—he shakes my hand of all things and introduces himself to me. There is nothing they can do but give me darvan—a pain killer—but that doesn't help, or helps not enough.

Wait around, then go to lunch—had two portions of meat loaf but there were no sandwhiches that i could keep for supper. Came back and waited again, reading a little bit. Then bill shows up and i walk him back to the gate. He is still as bouncy as ever and will be going to california in a few weeks—is taking his driving test on monday and i am jealous that i haven't learned how to drive. The folks don't come till a quarter to two.

We go to mays shopping for a hat again but they don't have any so they buy me a wild pair of bermudas as a gift from aunt pearl. I pick up two jazz records for 29 cents a piece—one of them has some stuff by mingus, gillespi and parker. Then we go see lover come back, a supposed comedy with doris day rock hudson and tony randall. Again a talky—some jokes but absolutely no use of the visual, or even music. Then we go back to mays.

Forgot to mention that first I go and pay off the candy store owner for the books that i stole. He thanked me for being so honest and i felt like a fool but i guess it felt good being honest. Went back to mays to look for a hat for mother—didn't find one. Thought it pretty rediculous for her to spend hard earned money for some frivlous little head warmer but i guess there are not too many pleasures in a life and looking good at a woman's luncheon is one of them. She still has beautiful legs—she's fifty now and still attractive. She was also wearing a new suit and i felt not the least bit guilty having them for the movies. Then went to whelans but didn't want to buy any food for fear of a tummy tum ache and the money that would be spent. Instead we stopped into a delicatessen and bought some salmon and olives I'll have for breakfast. Mother was having a headache so thought we ought to stop at shirley clement [*friends*] so we did. Alan was home as was tony and shirley and their little baby andrew and their dog collette. It was good to see a happy family functioning together. They were having filet mignon and offered me one so i sat down and ate. It was good. Alan lent me a book on "the worldly Philosophers" by Heilbroner about econom- ics. He is studying at Queens and sometimes like next week used my room to study in. We left and came back and then talked in the car some about tomorrow. Came back, did a little showing off and then went into donnies room to hear the records—they are great. Then Ed came in around nine and played Richter playing Schumann. Some of the piano music was nice, some was boring. Then spent a good hour talking with bob about nothing in partic- ular. He loaned me a nice long scarf to keep my neck warm and i made a card for mother's day. A pretty happy day—the movie could have been better. Maybe tomorrow we'll see jules and jim. goodbye.

A pretty happy day— the movie could have been better.

sunday may 13 ten oclock

woke by nine had a bagel then read some papers. Then tried to relax my neck—got a hot water bottle form the new rounds doctor. It felt better. Read some of confessions of an Art Addict by Peggy Guggenheim. A nice rapid and honest style, it tells the story of her education, a subtle and seductious one and lots of fun. Listened to the jazz record and i think it has parker and gillespi. Then when i just decided to go to dinner jay shows up all smiles. He warns me that we are to spend the entire day home celebrating mother's day. We park and then decide to buy some flowers for momma so we go to queens boulevard. I made a remark that i'd probably trip over all the furniture and feel closed in. Get a big greeting from everyone and go into my room—what a madhouse. Books begetting books and as a sideline some records.

The house looks nice and prim and just not enough speace for everyone. Have some sour cream and cottage cheese and then phone up madelynne [*cousin*]. She was home and i said i was coming over—then she told me that she was going to see the premise at queens college so naturally i wanted to go too. But they didn't even want me to go to madelyines let alone a play. Scouted around the room for some books that i want to take back—can't take all of them so i make a list of those books that i think i will want at a latter date. Also listen to the well tempered clavier beautiful stuff. Then aunt pearl and uncle murray come.

For about the first fifteen minutes the talk is why they were late—a man tried to commit suicide on a rain station and so they were held up. Forgot to mention that i spoke to irma [*cousin*] on the phone. She let it slip that she had once seen a psych man and said it was the best investment that she ever made and has made her a better mother and wife—good. Extends an invitation to me to come down to where they are living and plan to take her up on it. We eat and it is a delishous roast beef with all the trimmings. Just as we finish aunt evelyn and uncle paul come and the place gets a little noicy so everyone moves out to the living room. The men talk about the stock market and the women follow mother into her room to see her wardrobe—jay is busy washing dishes and being a good son and i look up in the paper and see that there is a program about eastern philosophy—about "bind"—I turn it on and it is alan w. watts looking drunk as usual (he always reminds me of john sinclair) he talked about paradoxes and some about pychoanalysis and the fact that while you were aware of being aware you really couldn't be aware. Then he brought up archery and how the master spent five years teaching his hand to open and shoot the arrow without opening. I think the way to summarize it is, don't watch a boiling pot. but take pot.

Went back into my room and knew how well i looked (after dressing)—want to take a walk and aunt pearl takes it with me. Lectures me on how not to do too much which i agree with her. Then talks about how she got better and ascribes it to one day taking a cold shower and realizing that she wasn't sick any longer. Then she wants to see how i play bridge so she deals two hands and i do very well with out doing anything much. They all piled into the car and took me back. At the end i said i didn't know if the doctor would have wanted me to come home, which was unnecessary. Also asked dad for my 200 dollars but said i couldn't have it now. They let me off—I scrambled back and plopped everything down on the bed in time to watch rififfi by Jules Dassin. It was almost a silent movie and one part for thirty minutes was completely silent while they were robbing a jewel safe. In the end everyone gets killed off. The suspence was kept throughtout. then went to see marty and we went out into the back and walked over to low 3 and i whispered for marge—she came out and we joked and then got cold and here i am writing. Now to read some of the books i brought.

it is alan w. watts looking drunk as usual (he always reminds me of john sinclair) he talked about paradoxes and some about pychoanalysis and the fact that while you were aware of being aware you really couldn't be aware.

monday night may 14, 1962

again wake up had a breakfast and came back to watch the columbia lectures. Came back to the room and tried to sleep, then cleaned it up for the rounds doctors—really for myself. Said i had a good weekend—Fogel said fair or good. said good. Didn't go to o.t., stayed and tried to read the buddist book but got tired so i slept till twelves. Went to lunch and had some london broil—ate by myself. Came back and tried to read but wasn't really interested.

Went to my first newspaper meeting and enjoyed it. Volunteered to do the movie reviews and also the advertising column—nice little honours let's see if i can do them. It lasted till three and came back worrying about the group therapy. Played some ping pong with donnie. Then it was 3:30. Doctor Plaut was there, two amys, another girl and donnie and myra—dr. Plaut introduced me to everyone and then Dr. Siegel came in—he was the steongrapher and didn't say one word. I started the ball rolling by answering the doctor's question—if i had group therapy before and i explained how i benefited from Dr. Kramer's group but that she was only a psychologist and so did not feel as though she were as fully qualified. Also about how i said how can i trust anyone if they were all sick. Nobody said anything much so i remarked that one time we discussed the wanting to kill a parent and asked around if any of the girls ever wanted to. Two or three offered yes and myra said that her father once tried to kill her. Then after some more quiet dr. asked donnie what happened here at meetings and answered nothing it was a dud. I said i would get awful afraid if we all sat around saying nothing that i would feel much more alone than i did. Then brought up aunt pearl and how she wanted to know what brought me here and i said it was a whole bunch of things. The others all agreed we were stuck on how to define traumatic and i asked the dr.—she said there could be varying degrees. Then i brought up the matter of parents and if we would ever bring up children and why. Myra sort of agreed that she wouldn't want to contribute to a childs suffering and that it was a very huge job. She also said that her parents had tried their best only it was not enough. Then Gene Franzetti came in and somehow the topic got turned to finding a mate. He is a catholic and so said he would only marry once. I suggested trial marriages, that is, living with a person and then if you were both in love and wanted to have children— then get married. Nobody concurred. I also wanted to know what the big thing with oedipus was—why it was a crime to want to make it with the old lady. The others seemed to think that it would cloud up roles, and strengthen the inter family rivalry.

I know i talked a lot but i think that most of the time i was making sence. I kept questioning people and tried to be analytical. Donnie said that by my talking i doubled the amount said previously. I ate with him and was very pleased that during the session i could get him to say that he was going to get better from now on. Had a turkey casserole for supper and joked with donnie. Then as i was coming back amy stopped me and thanked me for what i had done at the meeting and asked me my age, saying that i had marvelous insight. I said i had it but still it didn't help. We discussed the fact that Sam's bringing up his religion was a stopper to further conversation.

Came back and went up to poetry but there was none started for a while and listened to some jazz but got bored (was dancing for a while with amy remsen and didn't get excited—was disappointed to say the least) so came back and they were playing a game of volleyball in the backyard so i joined them. The grass smelled delishous but i didn't want to stay too long. Came in and asked frank stallings the new patient if he wanted to play ping pong and we played three games and joked some. I try and talk to him but he is very withdrawn—he walks around the low as if he were hiding from the fbi—he wears sunglasses and a suit jacket all the time and just walks back and forth. He graduated from princeton and that is all i know about him.

Spoke to maryse and they were having bingo for a night activity so i came back to my room and read some more peggy guggenheim, and picked my toenails. Did i used to eat them? I can't seem to get the knack of it anymore. Also reworked some of my diary this mornng. Made an observation at the newspaper meeting that i could respect Dick Hayes even if i didn't like him or was jealous. Want to write a short story on heshy bodner and those few frenetic days i spent in san francisco when i was close to making a fortune selling dictionaries. now will read.

tuesday may 15, 1962

again forgot to wake up when i was supposed to. Finally got up and went to bridge class—listened to the lesson but don't know if i understood what was going on—played a few games of bridge and then got bored. Talked with helen and we hadn't spoken in a long time—she told me she was in a quandary whether to go back to her husband or marry bob. I said i hoped i hoped. Then went to my d.a. The first time i didn't have to lay a book down on the other chair.

She smiled as usual and then i asked if i was terribly manic at the group therapy yesterday—she said no, what i said made sence—I was a little anxious, that was all. Related how donnie tried to make friends and what amy said about me having insight and the dr. said now what about that. I replied that it was mostly intellectual and that now i would have to learn to live with my knowledge emotionally but that i still want to be a child and not make decisions etc. We talked mainly about the good things i was doing like enjoying the play in a game of ping pong and not just playing it to win. My growing relationship with bob, and my having foster parents. She said it would only be temporary for about six months and by that time i might be well enough and get along with them well enough to take on the home atmosphere.

Wanted to hear segovia but the old men on the ward were listening to some western— heard the last half hour. It moved me so that there were tears in my eyes at one point.

Left and went to lunch. Started eating alone but think bob joined me or i had seated myself at his table— can't really remember. O yes i sat down with bob and cindy and they were telling jokes and we all told funny jokes and had a good time. The lunch was a little inadequate but so what. Then went to dance therapy and had to sit on the sidelines a lot—think that has to do with the thorazine. Then came back to the low and read the newspapers—played a game of ping pong, no—volleyed with hy fliegel and then went for my movie interview—copied out what the programs are to be, one of them i did speedwrighting and it was fun, hope i can repeat it. Then came back and again played ping pong and waited till supper. Went and ate with marge cindy and georgia. Had a good time.

Came back and bob was tired as usual—thought up the idea of making some tea and coffee in the kitchen so bob did. Picked up miller's "black spring" and started reading—he really is like no other writer except what i want to write like.

Forgot to say that before supper i typed up a letter four pages long in response to sam ware's letter from creedmore. I included some of my better poems and hope that he will get better. I really feel quite lousy about his being there and nothing to do but maybe it isn't quite as bad as elmhurst and he does have a friend there and he can paint something—I couldn't or wasn't doing at elmhurst [*Elmhurst Hospital, site of Robert's first psychiatric hospitalization*]. The word is that he won't have to stay there very long,. Went to choral group and could actually sight read—it was exciting. after heard some of wotseck and it is great. Then went up to low 4 for dramatics but they were reading patty chaievsky which i didn't particularly want to do. Wanted to hear segovia but the old men on the ward were listening to some western—heard the last half hour. It moved me so that there were tears in my eyes at one point. Played tickle the tummy with marty and then we came back to my room and exchanged poems. He has some imagemaker with in him. He really liked my stuff and i was proud that is about it.

Poems

is there which now is here."

dwise alone

ays

the ti

to think
to not think
to love
ah that is the way.

mother mother mother dear

mother mother mother dear
why when you are always near
do I feel so absolutely un me
why by now can't you see
that the whole wide world is not just you and me?

out of one night into another

out of one night into another
hello father, goodbye mother
time flows through me and I
through time
a mime actor I watch from dead lands

Home is there which now is here

I used to write—"Home is there which now is here."
now I understand not headwise alone
that home is always home
& always exceptionally there.

meetings mount monstrous

meetings mount monstrous
on even the duck billed platypus
on every little iota
does there need to be a vote?
can't we just shelve some items
or shall this misery continue ad infinitum?

My own ivory tower to come home to

As I go to climb not marble steps
my door is locked
for i'm not at home
all of me's there—books i haven't time to read
    for i'll be busy borrowing more and more
    from the local libraries that are mostly closed
to the retirees, housebroken housefraus and children runaways
from
drug infested schools
    and of cource me
so I climb paperbacks in hand urgently needing the toilet and the
key the
key, wrong key again
must be freudian
aha the cat's awake will he pounce me now or wait till the night
better get your (de)claws in now old chap for tomorrow i'll be
gone

water details undetailed; unfreeze a steak heat more water
flick the FM on and stare at the paintings on the wall
("as if a guest were here—") this one i got for almost nothing a
long time
ago and this one a friend who was

Moby

on waves of unwonder
is the white behometh there?
in the deeps, the darks
watching, waiting
and spring so the seasons
there should be stars
sprinkling the skies
not a cloud
am I to mutely stand guard
as, as . . .
no against the wind even
I'll heave the sails
lurching if need be
cautious of the boom
tasting the salt spray
and now to the floating sway
of sleep
    so deep so deep

As another year washes over

As another year washes over
and each of us is getting older
the boulders that you've rolled away
tumble through other thickets
and once more the life student that you are
asks and receives;
wisdom, love, health
may not grow on trees
but watching trees grow aids all three
so happy another birthing day
mother our mother who art on earth

to dream

to dream
ah then to not dream
suddenly to not even waken to this
silly something of a world
and remembering those unlogical logical
machinations of a perfectly understandable world
cat—what dreams you must have or do you dream at all?
the nagging of the not haunts me
so that over and over the same is even day-dreamed
now awaken each tooth brushed
orange juice gulped, coffee downded
ready for this cold and autumnal day
and then another night unready for
those visions, delusions and hallucinations
I shall dream of dreams

love is a sometimes thing

love is a sometimes thing
a springtime dream
a boring summers heat
the exitation of real togetherness in the netherdress
    love is the shortest distance between two minds parallel
    only perhaps to

but if i said everything (and I can for I know)
what would be left
    would be but psychotherapy or that
    group therapy
    and then we might as well spend sundays dearest filling in the
        cross word puzzle left over from last week

can you remember dear how queer how very strange were our
meeting
    the first things we did, and said and didn't say or so
        you say i never wooed you
    and blue (in the nude) were the under parts of your eyes
        before we went crazy and lived too much
    and now our eyes are gone and in their place occasionally
we know that things are happening that I am here and
    you are there.

He must be retired now*

He must be retired now
on what G-d knows
but for years and years
he was chief zookeeper
of us young jews
a little man, he rose
to heights immense
for the fear of the Lord
rang from his breath
I wonder what he believed
if he believed
but he handed us a heritage
none of us was worthy of
we were just a wild pack
and he, he was a man of G-d
perhaps he was the Great good Jehova himself

(will my sons know such dignity?)

(* *The "He" of this poem is Dr. Emanuel H. Baron, our Hebrew*
School Teacher at Congregation Shaare Torah in Brooklyn.)

Without beginning, without end

Without beginning, without end,
Without past, without future.
A halo of light surrounds the world of law
We forget one another, quiet and pure
    altogether powerful and empty.
The emptiness is irradiated by the
    light of the heart and of heaven.
The water of the sea is smooth and
    mirrors the moon in its surface.
The clouds disappear in blue space;
    the mountains shine clear.
Consciousness reverts to contemplation;
    the moon-disk rests alone.

well winter is over

well winter is over—
the buds now on the trees
a lot of good it does to me
I still seem to suffer
from the fate of loneliness
and where is the tender touching princess?
after whom I seek
is it that I'm too meek?
trembling and empty,
for years now I've been floating
like the sea
rolling and moving
going no place
but going all the time

cherry buds spotted on the limbs

cherry buds spotted on the limbs
soon to drop and be gone
well that's Spring folks
time to close up shop

where's the man who put up that wall?

where's the man who put up that wall?
it's been and will be for a long time
there's no love in it but by god it's strong.

So another year

to MOTHER, MOTHER, MOTHER DEAR
So another year,
some more wear
very little tears
and even less fears.
After all isn't everything getting
      better and better?
Aren't the fetters
falling fast and full freedom
feasting fine?
I wonder—what this is all about.
But about you (don't feel sad, or bad)
there is no wonder—
Just the wonder of your being
The joy, the gleeing:
that you've infiltrated into our lives:
the hive you've kept humming
Called home (homey sweet home)
meanders through my memory
floating like foam
      on beer
So another year
one cheer?
no, more—mighty millions
for the mother, the so many women
and one
      named—Anne Neugeboren
      (September 19, 1964)

just now

just now,
some while ago
I met the carcass
of a little lost somekind bird
with little tufts of feather on feather
and this bird will never sing
will never ever have the chance to fly
with the wind
will never build a nest
will never woo a mate
why did this little thing of a thing
die dead in some unknown night,
some foreign land?

Spring has sprung

Spring has sprung
so greatly hung
are huge havoc
of mire and muck
speaks the springs return
as my heart burns
beastly for the come of a renaissance
a greeting cognizance
of greens growing great
now my mind moves towards a mate
all the cliches
fill up my days
spring shouts
in short bouts
of beauteous ways
why aren't there two Mays?

trees

    trees
terrify and threaten
tell thoughts
always arriving awkward times
rhyming wrong, rifting right
and green, no longer, no red
roaring wrongways into days
nights not so much
terrible beautiful trees
and trees.

thinking of seeing friends

thinking of seeing friends
when for so long without an end I have been without them
touching to feeling to being
listening and seeing
walking and talking
and remembering old times
little crimes
against teachers
remembering those loud yelling shouting preachers
of some god awful morality
remembering our fantasies, remembering reality
and the new worlds that can and may unfold
for those who are therefore bold
and the laughing and crying
the deep breaths and sighing
o to be in New York
with a head that is a cork
holding down excitement
when the whole world is one great big delightment.

Robert gave the next group of ten poems to our cousin Madeleine on the occasion of her graduation from Queens College, and her entry into the Peace Corps.

to the beautiful m.
some poems for your perusal
written for the occasion
by your loving cousin

February 7, 1964

Young princess of the Kew Gardens scene

Young princess of the Kew Gardens scene
now that you have got out from between
how do you like the sky
so low so high
and yourself
with so much wealth?

so it's time for some singing

so it's time for some singing
some dancing some celebrations
m is finally leaving the nation
and will be bringing
to some humans
light and love
and away and above
some lousy sermons

just ride the waves of sleep

just ride the waves of sleep
and fall into the deep
just dream of sex
remember Tom Mix
and play
the day
away

God is a three lettered word

God is a three lettered word
love four
and your spirit that of a bird;
soaring
roaring
into and out of trees,
that knows how to please
a God
in love

so what shall you do

so what shall you do
you gay girl of the books
shall I tell you tales of crooks
who rob themselves blue?
shall I tell you of my childhood
which you know too well
Shall I weave you remries of the old neighborhood
so bright will spring this spring
and you ain't gonna be in Queens neither
I'd love to spend this our too few time
gone and away from incestuous thoughts
and on to the nub of life the very prime
we could drink deep draughts
of whatever you have in the house
and call certain individuals by their names
which might be IMA LOUSE
if only they knew. But they are not to blame
The one to blame, if nothing happens,
is you my dear
for by now your wits are sharpened
have fear, but only enough to spirit your way
through the muck and mire
and spend each and every day
as if it were full of pluck and fire
you now know full well
enough to keep you out of blastard hell.

tell me sweet lass

tell me sweet lass
with your eyes burning bright
to what foreign countries are you flying to tonight?
do you see that mass
of mobbing peoples
most of them are creeples
so let them be.
And we?
We can fly through freedom
and become unnumb
become aware
of the dare
called life
strife?
not much of that please
my dear you've come through with ease

green with envy

green with envy
between the screaming ivy
nursing her anxiety
i speak two words—good luck

New York

New York
can be the talk
of the world, but baby
I think I've had it
and I don't mean maybe
so now that you're getting older
starting to laugh
at half
the things that once made you angry
New York is all grey
and you
are blue, red or yellow
so you better get out
forget all the louts
and build your way
and say
come what may
I'm all right Jack
to whomever would like to stab you in the back

all these many years upon years

all these many years upon years
you've been to me all ears
and suddenly over a long period of time
I decided to listen, and I heard!

of all the many years that have passed beween us

of all the many years that have passed between us
I remember earlier times the best
Those were the years that we would sit
talking and laughing and playing little games
and I remember walks and talks on topics huge and small
but out of this I remember all
the love that you would never leave rest

these years last past
I fear we've spent too much time in disagreement
in flights and fights of nothing much
where has the winter went?
and have we lost touch with the
things of love
that should last?

me I think these are troubled days
for me and my such sad rhymes

but I feel as if I were awakening to a whole new world of love
and like. Of fun and good times
and am finally with your love fighting my way out of this
meandering mass.

Love is the beginning

Love is the beginning
it is also the twinning
of two
who say I do
then do
so happy doing
(whilst I in celebration
gather in the dewing)

here's cheers

here's cheers
some tears
I don't know why
but the I
in me
wants to see
you two
so joyous
your voice
whistling
like a thistling
on a rose
which goes
ain't we great

to think

to think
to not think
to love
ah that is the way.

so the family's met the family

so the family's met the family
and soon you're going to tie that knot
and soon after that you're going to be traveling
and coming back
and life will assemble itself
by you not for you
so happy goings
you know what I, everyone wishes
is the very best of the very
so tarry not
set up what has to be set
and begin as you've done already
take down the barriers between
man and woman

lucky you

lucky you
just the two
eyes blue-
brown
down
around the mouth
just south
of those eyes
are two sunny skies
worth miles
of my verse
terse
or long
end of song

so you're off on a voyage

so you're off on a voyage
did you unpack everything?
a long sentimental journey
(do you remember, Jay, teaching me those words?)
to everywhere
but most of all
right there
within your souls
(wherever the hell they are)

listening to memories

listening to memories
i hear the sound of summer last
of saturdays spent with joy
and now to think
the two of you are shooting forth roots
and growing green with envy
i await (eagerly) the blossoms
that come each spring

listen to the children child running

listen to the children child running
watch the city turning over in their
        dreams
take a voyage on the ferry
and with thy wiffer smell the blossoming
        cherry
the merry month of may
is on her way, forever gone
and with it comes the way
of joyous june jumping july and august
        august
and so forth
hurray for love

all these words

all these words
are not birds
all the talk
can not equal a hawk
but then why hawks?
or knives and forks?
or anything times anything
since this is the only world I know
I'd hope to sew up a thing or two
like what is the world
but why should I bore you
tell me—you don't have to
I know you're happy
and that is enough to make
me shed this coat of nonsensical despair
and smell the ozone in the air.
When something whispers in my nose
I know it's time to see the smells
of yesterday tomorrows
and last weeks todays
my memory predicts only peace
and you you know
will live happily ever after

of all the beautiful girls

of all the beautiful girls
in this amazing world
who would have thought
that you could be caught
but the freedom of eyes
can answer 10,000 whys
and all the freedom
rejoices to know
that your beau
is our Jay

meandering to remember all the joys

meandering to remember all the joys
just the two, you me, of us running through
the currences that we as sibling boys
you'd teach me wonders from out neath the blue
you've always loved me so, like noone else I knew
knowing now, some of what you then taught me
I myself Robert Gary a (young) man grown free
I love to ramble thinking, living much
in around, through the days, the years we've spent
and now something new a Betsey beauty such
with whom you have so much enjoyment
appreciation, love, everything
(my love can only grow) I give a ring
to all the new joys, of these I sing

Letters, 1958-1976

In the fall of 1958, at the start of my senior year of college, I left home for the first time and lived in an apartment near Columbia University, at the corner of Broadway and West 107th Street (during my first three years I commuted to Columbia by subway). For the next eighteen years, when I was living in diverse places—Indiana, New York City, Long Island, California, France, and Massachusetts; and when Robert, too, was living in diverse places—in Queens, in California; and in various hospitals, residences, and apartments—we corresponded regularly.

We exchanged hundreds of letters. Of those I saved, I have chosen some three dozen, and have provided brief explanatory notes. As with The Hillside Diary, I have retained most of Robert's idiosyncratic mis-spellings.

J.N.

At the start of my senior year at Columbia, I went out for and joined the varsity (lightweight) football team. Our mother objected strenuously, and (even) telephoned the Dean of the College to try to get me removed from the team. Robert came to visit me often during this year, attending classes with me, staying over in my apartment, hanging out with me and my friends.

Oct 29, 1958

Brother Dear Brother,

I would have hurried sooner but I just got your letter today. The money is enclosed.

With 55 dollars removed that leaves you with 81.63 to your account (plus interest). I don't know if you realize it but your little football throw has raised a rucass around here. Prolonged discussions go on for hours about their "Joe College." It may have to come to the time when all money out of Martense will stop. But I don't think that will come yet. I happen to think that joining the football team was the best thing you have done in a long time and would like to see my "big" brother play sometime.

Do you want me to notify the "folks" that you are short on cash? Do you want me to send you any more (I earn at least 10 a week of which only four are needed—the the rest either gets spent on my delicate stomach or mind or just gets lost).

It would be advisable if you wanted money to drop in some time just for love and then the next night call for the money. or something like that—you know how to be lovable.

The Rabbi called some of the boys to join a club—it is the same thing as the Minnonheirs except that there are going to be Youth Services on Saturday mornings (I give the first and maybe the last sermon this coming holyday!) There is only one difference. Mr. Nugaborn is not the leader—tough luck.

I received my usual report card Friday.

I will be in NY Monday for "LOOK HOMEWARD ANGEL" in case that means anything.

That is all for now Joe College

Your everloving and enduring brother

Robert

I lost my job today!

Brother Dear Brother,

Oct 29,1958

I would have hurried sooner but I just got your letter today.The money is enclosed.

With 55 dollars removd that leaves you with 81.63 to your account(plus interest).I don't know if you realize it but your little footBall throw has raised a rucass around here.Prolonged discussions go on for hours about their"Joe Colledge".It may have to come to the time when all money out of Martense will stop.But I don't think that will come yet.I happen to think that joining the football team was te best thing you have done in a long time and would like to see my "big" broter play sometime.

Do you want me to notify the "folks" that you are short ons cash? Do you want me to send you any more (I earn at least 10 a week of only four are needed -the rest either gets sent on my delicate stomach or mind or just gets lost)

It would be advisable if you wanted money to drop in some time just fbr love and then the next night c ll for the money.or some thng like that you know how to be lovable.

The Rabbii called some of the boys to join a clug it is th same thing as the Minnnnonheirs exept that there are going to be Youth Services on saturday mornings(I give the firstand maybe the last serman this coming holyday!)There is only one difference.Mr.Nugaborn is not t the leader --tough luck .

I recieved my usual report card Friday.

I will be in NY Monday for "LOOK H MEW RD ANGEL" in case th at means anything.

That is about all for now. Jo Colledges

Your everloving and enduring   other
brÖe

Robert Neugehoren

lost my job today!

After I graduated from Columbia in June, 1959, I worked for eleven weeks aboard the Empire State III, a training ship for cadets from the New York State Maritime College—I was assistant to the ship's Executive Officer, in charge of the ship's office. Our itinerary took us to England, Norway, Spain, France, and the Madeira Islands. When we arrived at our first stop, Plymouth, England, a letter from Robert was waiting for me.

thurs. June 2? 1959

Good evening

It is evening here at Martense St. The morning mist has left and in its place has come the evening bitterness the time of sunsets. Soon it will be nightfall and then it will be dawn time when little catsfeet come on the dawn—but for now the sky is darkening. It is

kinna hot and I must keep all my shirts tightly buttoned (someday I'll tell you a funny story) all day long the fan turns round and round in its woof and the purring motor purrs on and on and then when the fan is shut off (click) the inner mind of the artist (that's me) keeps hearing a dull fanlike noise. And at supperdinercoming-home time we sit around the family table and munch and sipsoupnoisily and listen to the nothings (not being sweet they are not whispered) someone or other died today and then some little story which is told dramatically to illustrate the way life horrible life is merciless to those who have sacrificed their entire lives to god their country and their children—this modern generation just can't understand them. And comes the time to pick apart someone and as vultures who rrrip apart the dead carcass of a onceuponatime living animule the people rrrrip apart the life from a livingdead object. there must have been a time way back when these people were people or children and they must have laffed just because it was raining or because it was fun to laff but now is the time for rememberances of sometimes true always exaggerated tales of yesteryear and day.
    ****

I wonder where you are now are you in that country called Englandscotlandandwalesandireland the places i learned all about in the ninth grade when I did my unit and got a ninety for the term. It must be beautiful from what I hear.
    ******

I was reading some of Walt Whitman the great American poet and nurse and the poems I read were nothing like o captain my captain our fearful trip is done (the captain in the poem is really Abraham Lincoln whom Whitman was in love with—you see it is an Allegory)—well anyway the poems i read were all about love. Gee you should see some of the words—the dictionary got all of them and it is very dirty.
    *****

Jan [*my girlfriend*] called yesterday and I guess she is lonely because she talked awfully long to me and she kept mentioning you.

My report card is

English—90 the bastard

Economics—90 what do you expect from an old newdealer

French—55 changed to 65 after 76 on the regents

Chemistry—55 changed to 65 after a 76 on the regents

Math—55 changed to 55 after a 57 on the regents

since a lot of other brilliant precosious youngsters flunked out the state of New York may pass some of them including your precosious brother.

I get my college boards marks tomorrow.

Marna leaves tomorrow and tonight is the last night that we will see each other and this puppy is almost panting.

I have to leave now. sorry for the long description of brooklyn but I thought you would like it being that you are in Europe you sin of a gun.

                    bothre
                    brothere
                    brotherb
                    boobby
                    bobby

i forgot to check spelling and etc.

*In the fall of 1959, after my return from Europe, I began grad-
uate study at Indiana University, in Bloomington (my first sojourn
west of New Jersey; by the end of the year I would drop out and
take a job in Indianapolis). Shortly after I left for Bloomington that
fall, Robert left Brooklyn (though he would return most weekends)
for Queens. Our mother, determined to find a new home, sent
Robert on ahead so that he would not have to transfer high schools
mid-semester, to live with our Aunt Evelyn and Uncle Paul and
their four children (Madeleine, Stephen, Martin, and Susan).*

[*Fall, 1959*]

Salutations from brooklyn,

Ah the world is wonderful the very air i breathe tastes. That
lovely girl Marna is no longer my true and only love. But don't feel
bad cheer up. It was my decision and glad i am for it. Our relationship was too restrictive and false and habitforming. The easiest
thing in the world was a usual conversation of the merits of critics
and latin versus modern poetry. The hardest thing was to actually
read. To actually feel. Someday perhaps i will grow to love her but
not now when the very earth shakes at my command when the very
sun rises and sets for me no not to be told by my love the sunlight
this morning was inebriating it touched my skin you know pat says
and father says and Mr. So and so authority of…I wasn't responding to her love calls and traps. You have grown so much well and
she saw it coming and tried to stop it anyway she could but i…I
thank her for a year spent nicely and an adolescence that i grew up
in and learnt about a lot of things but as of now we aint compatable. So there goes Marna. She was a beautiful girl.

I am now paying for my own shirts shoes and cleaning. It does-
n't bother me in the least except to know that my mind is obsessed
with these petty nuances. Our parents are so helpless poor mother
father was bankrupt in business and she was bankrupt as a mother.
They threaten everything imaginable but since there is nothing to
threaten they pretend heartrending sobs and rages and psychiatrists
and it looks like life will always be the same for some people.

Salutations from brooklyn,

Ah the world is wonderful the very
air i brethee tastes.That lovely girl marna is no longer
my true and only love. But don't feel bad cheer up.It was my
desision and glad i am for it.Our relationship was too restrictive
and false and habitforming.The easiest thing in the world was
a usual conversation of the merits of critics and latin versud
modern poetry.The hardest thing was to actually read.To actually
feel. Someday perhaps i will grow to love her but not now when
the very earth shakes at my command when the very sun rises and
sets for me no not to be told by my love the sunlight this morning
was inebriating it touched my skin you know pat says and father
says and "r.Soandso authority of... I wasn't responding to her
love calls and traps. You have grown so much well she saw it
coming and tried to stop it anyway she could but i ..i thank
her for a year spent nicely and a adolecence that i grew up in
and learnt about alot of things but as of now we a int compatable
So there goes marna . She was a beuatiful girl.

I am now paying for my own shirtsshoes
and cleaning.It doesn't bother me in the least except to know
that my mind is obsessed with these petty nuances.Our parents
are so helpless poor mother father was bankrupt in buissness
and she was bankrupt as a mother.They threaten everything imaginable but since there is nothing to threaten they pretend
heartrending sobs and rages and pysiatrists and it looks
like life will always be the same for some people.

Right now i don't really know what my philosophy of life is and i don't really care. I live and improve and learn. I just hope my ego doesn't split in two or something.

Alan [*cousin*] sent me a note and i sent him one but haven't mailed it yet. Was at John Steinbecks the other night--you know that decadent author. Let us see what else is new nothing but then too nothing is really ever new we live in an antique shop midst thousands of cliches and anachronisms and phony jewels every so often some jewel gets lost and is happily shining everafter in someones lucky lap.

I think that will be all. Thanks for the letter and write oftenly. Everyonce in a while i will be glad to send you stuff since every artist needs an audience you can be my understanding public.

brother bobby

Mon Sept 21, 1959

goodevening brother and it is evening here—you are probably eating write now and when you receive
—that was mother's single spacing—saving paper i guess

I haven't written to you mainly because i have changed a little—"sound the horn blow the trumpets" yes virginia darling there is no god and there is a state scholarship test. After one wild weekend whereby i managed to spend all the hard earned moneies that i earned last week (apprx 17$ more or less) in about ten taxi cabs and a broadwayoffbeat enemy of the people and then a dinner at tom steinbeck's home. No john wasn't home you see he isn't married to tom's mother anymore. Well anyway after all that drinking and revelry i gave up revelry and my true love and i am now studying. It is one of those all or nothing gambits and i hope that i can play it well.

Nothing is really knew except for the fortieth time i was told that i would have to wipe my own snotnose and that it was just a shame that two people wasted their hardearned lives on two anti-semites who spend their time reading and listening to good music and out at plays and parties till don't get me wrong the most i wish for you is that you have a good time and that...

aw what's the use u must know the line better than i.

I am in the midst of rediscovering life reading and eating and breathing and talking and thinking you know like jean shepard i guess.

by the way i read some where that cinema 16 was going to show an experimental film entitled Shadows *– if i receive a ticket i will be sure to ask for my five dollars and send to no i think i will take some smart jewish girl and tell her all about my wretched sufferings my arts and then shake hands with her as i leave her at her doorstep.

well i must get back to the books (the great conversation!) you know it would be nice to hear from my struggling brother—saw a poem by louis simpson it is in the american scholar summer 59 if you care.

au revoir and you know that everynight that i puked i did so i could get attention and wake you up it was my way of getting of loving you after all sometimes i spent two shifts a day at play.

with fond remembraces

frere

On Sunday nights, Robert and I would lie in bed listening to Jean Shepherd's radio program together. One time, after listening to an interview he did with John Cassavetes, we chipped in and sent money to Cassavetes (Robert writes $5—my memory says $10) to help him produce his experimental film Shadows.

business letter

I am going to Antioch if I can help it. You go to school for three months and then you go to work for three months. Tuition is $1000 and expenses for a typical year come to $1501 plus 265 which equals 1776$ which isn't too much considering that you work for half the year and can save something I guess.

I have three choices for college—Antioch will be one—you suggest two others brother dear i need to know by october fourth please write via special delivery. It is one of those three shots for a quarter spend the rest of your life in minute installments deals.

I am enclosing a letter written some time ago which was written whilst i was in the depths but not correcting anything though. Am reading like mad and doing passe in school. See no reason why i shouldn't pull a 90-94 average i only have Math 6 (just got transferred back to my beautiful smart and now married last years fucking teacher, met her in the village at some movie house and can't remember for the life of me whether she was with her hubby or not) then i have Am. History 7 which shold be quite a breeze for an old radical turned------. Next comes physics which strangely i find enthusing—it replaces that vacuum left by superstition and etc. And next we have creative writing which deserves at least a 97 they are finally printing something maybe.

Received the Columbia Forum today. Can I send a note to them giving then your address and asking to send a copy to me? I should like to receive it.

Reading something by Jacques Barzun.

Lets See Whom did I meet this weekend. o just some leaders like the entire youth movement from that organization—the Rest of the weekend was spent at the movies. Saw The Informer, Love in the Afternoon, Susan Slept Here and something with jerry lewis that i walked out of after the first 2 and a half minutes.

If you have 36 cents and 1 and a quarter hours riding the subways or something pick up a copy of the fume of poppies by jonathan kozol—he is 22 and just graduated from harvard

that is it since i must get back to joyce checov darwin falling bodies and accelerated motion harpers the new yorker barrabas the odyssey and somewhere after some 12 teas sleep and then a cold cold shower and then good morning it is a brite new day.

Daddy is a manager now you ought to write to him and your brother read your missle from lush country but it was two thousand pages in back of me so don't ask me what you said although it seems like your playing tennis with virgins [*my girlfriend's name was Virginia*] and sleeping with arnee [*my old college roommate, now in Bloomington*] or something

brother

In February 1960, while in his senior year of high school, Robert decided to move out of our parents' apartment. He left Queens and moved in with several other young men in an apartment on Manhattan's Upper West Side. Our parents urged me to fly home from Indiana so that I could urge Robert to move back home. They paid for my flight east, and though, as I wrote in Imagining Robert, *"I was proud of Robert for having done what most teenagers fantasized but few risked, I found myself working to perusade him to move back to Queens, and to our parents' apartment, at least until he could, in four months, graduate from high school." When, on my fourth day in New York, he told me he had decided to move back home, "I had the sickening feeling I had won a battle I did not want to be part of—that I had done my parents' dirty work (again?)," I wrote, "pressuring [Robert] into being somebody he didn't want to be, and into doing something that, no matter my sensible rationalizations, he doubtless felt (toward me as well as toward them) as submission and defeat."*

When I returned to Indiana, I stopped attending classes, and spent most of my waking hours in my dormitory room working on a new novel. By May I decided to drop out of graduate school. To support myself—and my writing—I took a job at a Chevrolet plant in Indianapolis as a Junior Executive Trainee for the General Motors Corporation.

Sun May 2- 1960

dear brother jay,

I have been doing next to nothing. I have alienated almost all friends—including reading and writing. About the only things I still do are those things necessary to a young boy. These things when I do do them are indulged in but even they are waning. So sorry the progress report for what ever the heck the date is would have to report—chronic bewilderment and sence of wonder setting in, occasional periods of intense desire slackening off into long periods of apparent nothingness.

all seriousness aside,

well it is spring for a while anyway and everyday is like a new-day really olded and ended by the day or night in the bright land after sunglasses have been removed.

(please don't worry)

I think that your earning 475 a week is great I never heard of anything so fantastic. A note to take note of in a few years is that the per capita of a place like porto rico is 500 smakeroos A YEAR in other places it is even less. Well good luck and please don't ever feel obligated to send any of that to your poor big city brother who is continuing his fight against almost all odds to create some beauty out of a grey world. Please don't feel obligated in any way.

How is your social life?

And how are you feeling?

love brother robert.

Monday

Dear Jay

Please disregard the foregoing letter. However since I wrote it and it would be dishonest if I tore it up as not being any part of me I shall send it along anyway.

Everything is really great. I would now like some information from you.

1. The Columbia University Forum. Please arrange for me to get it. (Or authorize for me to send a change of address to Flushing).

2. Apprx. how much do you think I should ask from the folks in expence for the next year. We have come to some sort of agreement (thank heavens for social workers) now all I have to do is ask for lets say $2 a week and promise to go to schul on Sats. So I would like to know approx. how much you spent commuting etc.

3. how many rooms in your apt.

4. do you ever read any of those new york only type things like Partisan Review of Commentary? (reason for Commentary is you mentioned Fiedler)

5. what is love.

6. Do you think it was silly to go to [*Camp*] Winsoki as usual—
I rationalized everyway (the folks are quite obnoxious now they
are not allowed to make me do things (o gee officer krupke krupe
you) but there is no law against needling—so
we'll spend the summer in the
hot city—but I really figured
out that just like I
returned home at sixteen
at sixteen the only thing
I could do wd be to
work in a camp. Now
isn't it a little ridicu-
lous to work in any
place that you are
going to hate so you
might as well pick one
where hate is impossi-
ble (if only I will
remember that in the
middle of july) ergo—a
whole summer living off
the fat of the land. Even if
things really turn out ok
creating a daily newspaper for
which there is no other reason
than a vague sorta hope to convert the
barrel to rotten Jewish pickles (a cucumber does not taste anything
like a pickled cucumber).

I had some real questions like am I really sane and really talented and some other unimportant things but well we can't remember
everything.

anyway have a nice cool summer and be sure to open a bank
account and by the way rich brother I am graduating from high
school

love
robert. (brother)

XYZ—I am starting to write and think again.

In the fall of 1960, while I was still living in Indianapolis and
working for General Motors, Robert, having won a New York State
Regents Scholarship, began his freshman year at the City College of
New York.

[*Fall, 1960*]

dear jay,

I really do not know where to start. Where should I start? And
where should I stop? I have decided, for the moment, to stop living
in Queens, and will soon be living in Manhattan. I shall start cul-
ture program for the culturization of Robert Neugeboren, Gary. I
was tres disturbed after I phoned you because I remembered that I
had not asked the question of myself—why did I call you? It was-
n't for money, for that I know you'd say look robert if you act in a
way, a way that seems right to me I send along some cash. Well that
is perhaps one of the reasons I am "moving," I am tired of acting
nicely I should like to be good. Money should have nothing to do
with goodness. For advice? No, because I am now at a position
where I want and need to do what I need to do. No matter what
other people think. Probably I called just to hear if you were alive,
alive as you always have been to me. Probably and maybe not. Next
time I use Mr. Bells system of hari-kari it shall be after seven if I can
remember.

Once started I know not where to go. O lord lead me through
valleys, grey canyons, halls of whorey life, and lord, my lord, I am
mine servant.

Life now now something which seems part of me. And Henry
Miller and N. West and Bill Shakespeare and Picasso, Modigliani,
Shahn, arp, Brancusi, Freud, Faulkner, Castro, Nixon, Stevenson,
Chaucer, bread, the ancient Greeks, $f(x) = $ me. The rain, Harlem,
the Fall, the rivers of New York, the blue sky, burning sun, and the
people people pick their places in my heart. J'espere la langue de
francais sera mine bientot. The film form flunks.

And I don't keep on living. Some days are born all to their,
themselves I stopped living some years aback I think, I started loving then. I stopped smoking some time ago for lack of interest and
restless I became when cancer started creeping through my lungs.

Send my love to anything you love, for if you love it then I love it for you. For everyone except yourself I might hold different opinions, but you Mr. Neugeboren are a case that strikes as being quite interesting. If you like you can consult me for an hour a week at which time we shall review your life and come to grips with certain gripping problems. What—you have no problems?

In gym we are wrestling. At first I sort of thought of it as only (?) a kafka type dream. We go into this cage and half and full nelson with people we don't even know, or hate. But by now, I have forgotten that the boy (or man) that I wrestle with is really anyone, he is everyone and everyone has no feelings or if he does He doesn't show so. So I guess the guidance personnel director would say that my interpersonal relationships are improving. I could agree or disagree. In fact I don't give one hoot about him, or his wife and children.

My friends are as usual doing better than I. Or at least they seem to be. Marty Kaiser jumped through a plate glass window because the glass was trying to believe it wasn't there. Marty, a believer, had faith and when he wasn't looking the invisible curtain shattered on him. He wasn't hurt much (?) but now has a funny mark. He always had a scar on his farhead (in fact the first time I met him was after seeing Wilder's "skin of our teeth," I asked if he was cain.) well now he has a cross on his farhead which is really new anyway since he has always been a good christian. (sign +). He met James Thurber Kol Nidre night (It seems the [*Frank*] Loessers were holding one of those get togethers and to get the Jews off the streets the Kermit Bloomgartners, these and the Kaisers were invited.) Anyway, Marty said that Thurber was still alive and still saw, which was very incouraging—most of my "gang" or followers have remained in the city (or rather Brooklyn) and fighting their own and the worlds problems. I don't want to drop names if you like you can ask me a question about someone and I will be then glad to answer it. Sue is working like picasso at Cooper [*Union*] and having as much fun as usual. I don't think I told you about Jenny. We parted. She went back to the Hebrews and I to the bohemians and never did the twain meet. It wasn't messy or anything, we both knew what had to be and so we beed. She was/is really beautiful and (is) perceptive and percosious and in love with most of things in her her world. Her world was not my world, and i doubt she was in love with me. So she took one train and I the other and what can I say?

CCNY is beautiful. The people are beautiful. The girls are amazing, and I am making contacts with lots and lots of people who I would like to contact.

other wise things are as usual and I hope America gets a chance to read your words. Once again feel free to write . . .

robert

hope to be seeing you, your words and Virginia here in New York (the communications capital of the world) soon. Soon, before your contract with General Motors expires anyway.

Robert

read some of Uses of the Past. Mr. Muller is human, and sometimes speaks like humans should speak about humanity.

dear brother and jay,

(I address you so for the obvious reason(s) that being you will always be my brother, till death do us part and even past, you may not always be jay, already as a writer you have rebecome j.m.neugeboren a being which i never knew)

things are things here at—flushing, kewgardens and queens. Kennedy stll seems to be the president elect, although he may never get there. The mails have become electronified with a machine reading and sending all messages any and everywhere in a matter of seconds—the mailers however are not doing so or as well tusseling with the law and god and themselves.

I myself am floroshing if nothing else

School seems so silly, sipid and academic.

Money is pouring in from heaven and other places. The guggy [*Robert was working at the newly opened Guggenheim Museum*] still a beehive for americans has seen fit to remploy me and my services. And the chics in greenich village now get their wall st. jnl, h. trib. and n.y.times courtesy of r.g.n. (I have some [*Daily*] mirrors, one of which I have been instructed to slip under the door). It was a good job in that I learnt how to ride a bike and now can. Also saw many sunrisings over manhattan. Also did not get much sleep, got mucho money however and the thrilling sensation of riding right railing raming and running up a down one way st,. with a Fresh plucked jersey chicken truck raming and puking his way down the other end. (or down, folks) In washington's Heights, to which I have climbed i will soon leave. Leave behind perhaps the derriere-garde of this modern generation.

and past imaging how blind these "modern" kids are. Well, I am not. What else? Nothing else.

Everything else.

Saw The Apartment, so did the folks on my recommendation (they saw it before me, but seem to have seen a different version, thought it was ok nothing else) will see it again, no, like any great artwork am always seeing it. Hope you saw E. O. Neils iceman who came. Sidney lumet is a horrible director but jason was great, also eugene, also sorrell booke who was more than good. Seeing sorrell sort of shut me up in a world four years ago. What a world. our town is no longer our town, and people then are no longer here and now I am in colledge. Hurrah for progress. [*In 1958, Robert played Wally Webb in a Sorrell Booke-directed Columbia Players version of Our Town*]

Am sorry that the American publishers of J. M. Neugeboren are stinkers.

The great state of new york has sent me money and threatens to take three hundred dollars for my education starting next year. I will first go out on strike before I pay to be educated. Rocky is cookie. Let us hope that the full face of Job (alias Jack, Franklin, Jesus, brother, son, lover, and husband and to bubling birthing jacquelyn and all america living in peace and harmony striving and struggling with labor pains, and civil pains and democracy pains and pain pains) Kennedy. is as courageous as some of his profiles.

Now there is nothing else, except tomorrow and tomorrow is thanksgiving, so happy bird day, happy day day and happy ginny if she is still by your side. With some of the best wished wishes in the world (east of chicargo)

I remain   robet ccny 64?

In early January, 1961, shortly after I had quit my job at General Motors, and was about to drive across country and stay with cousins in California with whom Robert had stayed many years before (he and our mother traveled there together, by train, when Robert was seven years old), Robert, now living on West 89th Street in New York City, sent me a five page Special Delivery hand-written letter on 5-by-8 lined paper. On the front of the envelope he wrote: "ATTN: whoever cares the subject matter herein is as unim-portant as your next breath," and on the back "hurry hurry."

[January, 1961]

Dear Jay
what can I write? I don't even
know if I know
whom you are
that I adress, myself to(o)

and the words that I ink
down, shall reach out and touch
your mind
and where will your mind
be,
in some sea
of a country
far from me
whomever however I know not whom
I am
sence nonsence
what?

calif. here you come
why? o.k. visit H. Miller and
the pacific (important, stop, mother received news from Circles
cousins
they say send Jay on we welcome him,
but the pacific sea should fill
your bladder, and jelled yes
and all of you
and not traveling, have fun
    anyway
and every day
O.K. so I owe you lots and lots
of mail
    but why
    ?
    there is nothing to say
    or not

except the sky was blue before
and soon shall see another dawn
(another year, good cheer)
still and
mourning for some flighty
                    night
–and once again writer brother
I ask not are you right
    I ask nothing
You must have some questions
    I am not Kafka (!), Joyce
Cummings, sans everyoldone
    I am me
    I am me
Robert Gary Neugeboren
for reasons beyond the control
of everyall (terrifying times)
    I hasn't writing
but all shall be different
    tomorrow,
pooh!
    a winnie-the-pooh
    and way of you
and snow
    and
                friends
and
    hello
goodbye
                but enough jibber
jabber
now to read
    (to reach)
to heed the word
    (teach the world)
    and
happily newsyear
love go ginnie

love to you
*most of all love to myself

Some New Poems, older than last weeks soft snow
I
memories lie
like histories
which would die
if people weren't afraid
to break their staid
corages
and spare their children
(tiny billions) from a fate
the same again as them.
III A QUEStion
what is tiredness
but an everyday death
- holding one's breath
from life
    from life

II A FRAGMENT, Blunted
half awake until nolonger
No longer
    Less stronger
    and more blind
        to be
        see
a path of sky
blue high, glancing dancing off
        some window
a snow drop praning

A half year later, in June, 1961, Robert drove across the country, to California, with a friend. A few months before this, our mother had taken him to see Dr. Oppenheimer, Senior Psychiatrist for Adolescent Services at Kings County Hospital. Dr. Oppenheimer advised our mother to have Robert hospitalized immediately, and she told me that Dr. Oppenheimer said Robert would never be able to live outside a hospital. I convinced Robert to get another evaluation. Milton Klein, our friend and neighbor at 221 Martense Street, then getting his Ph. D. in Psychology, arranged for an evaluation by Dr. Robert Gould, Director of Adolescent Services at Bellevue. The result: Dr. Gould saw no reason for Robert to be hospitalized, and said that he did not even think Robert needed psychotherapy. From Los Angeles, on June 26, 1961, Robert sent the following letter to our parents (a note to our letter carrier— "Hello Joe"—on the front of the envelope).

[*June, 1961*]

dear everyall
well.
and after that there must be much to say. Yes I did receive your letter this morning mother and I really appreciate the change in spirit that has come over the Neugeboren family. First you all being nice and rested and then not being so g-damned troubled with the thousand little formalities of death. Also (and up to here you may have been agreeing with me now you will protest) your almost acceptance that I know what I am doing. Which is wonderful because dr. oppenheimer and his sicknesses aside i doubt if i shall ever be knowing what I am, or what I am doing. But yes hillside inc. i shall be able to function, and with the passing of some time you may even think that I am functioning well.

All that was just to let you know that no great change has come over me, and that I have not been overcome by this beautifully corrupted town—corrupted you answer? Yeah corroded by the sun and salted sea and all those one time humans whom are now free to frequent life and other things that those of new york have heard so much about (about oranges you can still buy them in supermarkets and there are palm trees but they seem to grow no fruits)

Speaking of time, in the city, after how weeks now of travelling? I have just received a postcard from sue speaking that they will have time to write me sometime next week—you people are sick.

I am somewhat afraid to start writing down EVERYTHING that happened to happen in America while I was travelling, but for sure certain I learned more than a hell or heaven of a lot and haven't stopped yet. I'll probably go at my memoirs sometime next week and if the circles are really as nice as they say stay there for life (That is a joke). Blanche called this morning to apologize for "Ritchie" [*Blanche's son*] being out of town—gosh mommy your friends must think I have nothing to do in this world besides go crazy, anyway she made a dinner with/for me tomorrow eve with ritch, and dave and her I think she was very nice trying not to wake me up.

(even with all children being beautiful Roberta Cohen is some sort of movie star or at least a nasofer, aunt ethel shold be more than a proud grandmaman) had a first birthday wednesday. I'll bring the baby a reptile I think.

About writing procedures you can either mail things here (speak. of things thanks for the clothes they are hansome or I am hansome) or

ROBERT GARY Neugeboren
c/o General Delivery
Berkeley Californika

I think we will be there for aprx a week but marty rides the truck and i do not even want to get annoyed. He says that yhou should send mail here but i tend to think that we will be gone for a while.

Needless to say I think it is a very good idea that all four of us are still, or maybe beginning to communicate, and after looking at millions of these lost kids and older kids (the older of adulted kids do what?) I know that now that most of all our problems etc came from the factation that we loved each another too much and people prefer hate.

Also needless thank you for your mail and money
and also love

robert (everywhere i wander people name me neugy and they all strangely think they are original bah on them)

if possible could you jay send some of my love to aunt mary and use your discretion about i wearing ritchards [*Mary's son, who died, in 1959, at age 17, of muscular dystrophy*] sweater and meeting some wonderful people thereby. I also really remembered him and sort of traced a few of my good character traits to his remarkabley optimistic always attitude.

also someone in the home call sue klein and say a few words on how i couldn't write but will within the next day or so.

love again

dear everyall,

well.
and after that there must be much to say.Yes I did recieve you
r letter this morning mother and I really appreciate the
change in spirit that has come over he Neugeboren family.First yo
u all being nice and rested and then not being so g-damned troubl
ed with the thousand little formalities of death.Also (and uo
to here you may have been agreeing with me now you will protest)
your almost acceptance that I know what I am doing.Which is wonde
rful because dr. oppenheimer and his sicknesses aside i doubt
if i shall ever be knowing what i am,or what I am doing.But yes
hillside inc. i shall be able to function,and with the passing of
some time you may even think that I am functioning well.

All that was just to let you know that no great change has come
over me,and that I have not been ovecome by this beautifullycorru
pted town-corrupted you answer?Yeah corroded by the sun and salte
ed sea and all those one time humans whom are now free to
frequent life and o her things that those of new york have heard
so muc about(about oranges you still buy,then in supermarkets
and there are palm trees but they seem to grow no fruits)

Speaking of time,in the city,after how weeks now of travelling
2i have just received a postcard from sue speaking that they
wi ll have time to write me sometime next week-you people are
sick.
I am somewhat afraid to start writting down EVERYTHING that
happened to happen in america while I was travelling,but for sue
e certain I learnned more than a hell of a lot and haven't stoppe
d yet.I'll probably go at my memoirs sometime next week and if the
circles are really as nice as they say stay there for life(that is
a joke).Blanche called this morning to apolizize for "Ritchie"
being out of town-gosh momm y your friends must think I have noth
ing to do in this world besides go or azy,anyway she made a dinner

Robert returned from California in the late autumn of 1961, and moved back in with our parents in Queens. (I was, by then, living in Teaneck, New Jersey, and teaching at the Saddle River Country Day School). In early February, 1962, following a psychotic episode in which, among other things, he tried to kill our father and fantasized (on the way to the emergency ward) that he was being taken to my funeral, Robert was hospitalized on the psychiatric ward at Elmhurst Hospital in Queens. From Elmhurst, in late March, he moved to Hillside Hospital.

Here follow several letters he wrote from Hillside—the first two to me, two months after the Hillside Diary ends (when I had returned to Bloomington, after a two-year hiatus, to complete my Masters Degree), and the others, nearly a year later, to our father, who, in early February, 1963, suffered a heart attack and was hospitalized. (When my mother called and told me to take a plane east immediately, she also told me that our father was not expected to survive the night.)

Our father survived this heart attack, and lived for another 13 years. (He died in Florida in 1976, at the age of 72, of emphysema.) In one of his letters to our father—while our father was still in the hospital—Robert writes, "I do not know if some of the sparkle has been taken out of my life by psychotherapy but I do know that I am much more realistic and much happier."

[*Summer, 1962*]

Dear Jay

there are no porcupines here and i miss their quills so i use my typewriter knowing fully well that working with machines slowly and surly makes one himself into a senceless machine. But i am lazy like so many other Americans who live in the age of anxiety but i am not anxious because i have the pleasure every evening of wiping away my feelings with the taking of some drugs. So your favorite brother is not only an emotionally disturbed mentle patient but also a drug addict. I have been born a jew but of late have become a catholic going to confession twice a week.

I interrupted the letter for a few games of bridge and some sleep. I really wonder what happens when we sleep.

I received batches of mail yesterday and there is nothing i like better in the world, excepting a good fuck, then receiving mail from friends and family. I got a letter from San Francisco and it was a very nice letter.

I really think that before coming home you should see the country like the grand canyon, las vegas, and then the coast and mexico and then the north west which i hear is beautiful country. Really jay you haven't taken any vacation this year and i do think that a trip to the west coast and your meeting some great people would be just the thing. But that of cource is your decision.

Yesterday i started my new job as an assistant to the medical librarian and i goofed off for the first day but it was fun he let me loose in the library which was great. I am also writing up my creative therapy painting and reading rabelais. He is quite funny only my reading is very slow although i am learning to skip parts which is encouraging. today is friday so that makes this a three day letter. I just put up a mobile that i made in o.t. and it is great the thing really moves. It is a combination of wires, copper enamelled plates, and string. I had a rather trying day and as of now am only getting saterday off but the doctor is going to come around again so we shall see what happens.

I haven't been writing as much as I discontinued my diary but i hope to work on some stories if i ever get around to them, also again i would like to send out some of my poetry.

It is very hot here and i feel like a clam only i wear clothes and have my hair combed my teeth which i never brush miraculously stay in my mouth for some reason. Do eyes grow or do they remain the same size from childbirth a question. I read the mole and didn't particularly think it great. I always wonder in that type of story who the narrator is talking to—the reader?

A new newspaper came out today but it is so crappy that i don't think i'll send it.

that's it for today goombye

robert

[July 13, 1962]

Dear jay the student

I like to receive your letters but would rather have you here of cource. I want you to get your masters and if you want your phd. whatever the heck that is. I guess that is what my doctor has because i just found out today that he is a psychologist and not a psychiatrist. I may get a pass this weekend to go out by myself who knows. These last two days have been great i have been socializing much more with the patients and especially with some of the girl patients. I went out of the hospital on both nights and think that it is really good for my therapy since i am fighting back and being more aggressive. I went visiting tonight to a friend of the girl (amy) that i went out with. I learned tonight that she was coming to see the social worker and i was to go swimming. As i said above i am reading and writing less but having a good time which is i guess what i am supposed to do. Pretty soon some jazz is going to go on, my roommate is gone for i think the rest of the weekend so i have the room all to myself. My friends marty and jimmy are in the room and it has just been painted. Sneaked amy and candy into the room today and amy washed my hair it is soft and fluffy and really looks good.

i somehow want to thank you and ask you to stop at the same time all your compliments of me.

The jazz is great and at one tonight wbai is going to have a program on james agee which should be fun...I wrote some more poems i think this week and haven't started editing any of my stuff that is lying around. As i mentioned before they have painted my room this week and the colour is pretty noncommital miserable yellow piss colour...Went swimming this morning and it was very nice. I still sometimes wonder if anything is happening but i am having a good time and my doctors are good so i shouldn't complain.

I've been listening to more music and especially jazz. Music is quite enjoyable and emotional...I'd love to go to some jazz spot but of course I can't drink so...Dr. Kline is trying to get me to tell things again i hope he is successful. I think that is about all for tonite.

love robert gary

I got a copy of the Moviegoer am reading other stuff now so I'll save it. How is arnie & co?

February 18, 1963

Monday night

Dear Dad, It was really wonderful to see you yesterday looking in such great shape. I'm sure you do not like to stay in the hospital as much as and probably more than I. But we both have been overtaken by a sickness that we both know so little about. I trust however that the doctors and staff at each one of our hospitals knows exactly how to treat us. Perhaps I sound too clinical. But I know now as never before in my entire life that medical science is really as great as mother always told us. With each day here at the hospital I am getting stronger and healthier. I am enjoying more things and understanding more about myself and the world that surrounds me with I would say each hour. I am much less frightened now than I have ever been in a long time. The family conferences along with the rest of my therapy has helped me immencely. Yours and Mother's patience and good ready-to-learn attitude has told me time and again how glad I am to be your son.

I received a five page letter from Jay today telling me how happy he was to receive my last letter and I had to read through a great many compliments before he wrote about what he was doing and how he was having a good time. He mentions his students' papers with the same distaste that I'm sure his students write them in. But Jay says he can become satisfied when he knows that he is teaching his pupils things that they never realized before. I am sure that above it all he really enjoys teaching much more than he will admit. I think he would be much happier in New York and specifically at Columbia than he is at Indiana University but that may come next year. I know how much Jay would like me want to be near home and be able to see the family. But that shall come in time. One thing I am learning through therapy is that things take time. And for the first time in a long time I am in no rush about anything. Except of cource getting well. I think all of us patients would like to get out of the old hospitals and back in the world that we enjoy so much. Jay writes that he is painting and learning a great deal about it. I have been painting for the past eight or nine months and I haven't really disciplined myself so that I could learn much about the art of painting. But I have had fun and I have done some good work. I would like you to see some of my paintings for I think you would like the colour combinations and some of the shapes.

When I came back yesterday I didn't do very much. First before I got back Mommy and I ate at a delicatessen—it was nice but mother was concerned with getting me back to Hillside for she had some bug that I missed my medication. It was all cleared up at todays conference so there are no hard feelings left. That is what is so wonderful about the family conferences that I have learned that we can speak together and not let old gripes or grudges build up to a boiling point. I am doing more of this in my interpersonal (wow!) relations. I am learning an awful lot. Anyway when I came back I had dinner again—some chicken and then did some talking and walking and then went to see the "Grand Hotel" I had seen part of it once before, last year, but I had not seen very much of it. It was a fun picture and Greta Garbo and Joan Crawford were great to watch. So were John and Lionel Barrymore and all the other characters. Afterwards.... we settled down for a nice quiet game of Bridge. It was lots of fun—I am relearning how to play the game because I haven't played the game in months. It is very relaxing and entertaining. It is also some what of a challenge. I don't know if I like it better than chess for they are two different kinds of games. I have never played the little Pinochle that you taught me. But I am sure that I will someday. I went to bed early and had a nice nights sleep full of some of my favorite dreams. I don't remember many of them and my doctor is just as happy. He thinks we have better things to talk about than my dreams and I think he is right.

Today was a rather full day. I painted in the morning and had a newspaper meeting in the afternoon. We must have spent a whole half hour discussing how we should word goodbye greetings to patients. I refused to get involved with such a rediculous argument and did some doodles. Of all the freudian slips—I forgot to mention that we had a family conference at eleven. It wasn't much of a family conference without you and Mrs. Levine but I think we got quite a few things straightened out. I think mommy could probably tell you more about than I could write in fact it would probably take her two hours to tell what went on for 40 or 50 minutes of the conference. Of cource the doctors asked how you were and were very concerned about your health . . . . but to tell you what I am doing is not to tell you how I am feeling more about how fine I am feeling and much I miss you some more tomorrow for now good night

Tuesday: I have to go to an activity right now so I can't write much. Please know that I am constantly thinking of you and hoping that your progress will be as good in the next few days and weeks as I have been told and see up till now. I promise to write soon and even more important I promise both you and myself that I will get well soon.

lots of love
Robert

wednesday March 6, 1963

Dear Dad,

I was so glad to hear that you are coming home. That certainly was a short stay in the hospital. I hope by now you are well rested enough to be in comfort at home. I'm sure that mother will make you as comfortable as possible and bring you back into as good and healthy shape as is possible.

Nothing really special is happening here—except that I am getting well. I can feel it every day that I am coming more into the world that I live in and am learning from and enjoying it. Yesterday we had Dance Therapy an interpretative dancing session and I was feeling so good that I did a dance solo. It was much appreciated by all and all applauded. Some of the ham in me came out but I didn't go too far and make a fool out of myself another thing which I have learned here at Hillside—how to have appropriate behavior. It is raining some thing miserable today we again have great big floods and today the fire department was here to see about the electric wiring that may be getting wet. Right now they are pumping the flood from one side of the building to another which I do not see too much sence in doing but I guess that they know what they are doing.

I can't believe that the week has gone so fast here it is Wednesday already half the week over. It is amazing how fast time travels. We just decided that we are not putting on "Our Town" we will be putting on a farce instead something that everyone agreed to. The reason we're doing the farce (of which I don't know the name) is that it is shorter and funny. I would have liked to see us do such a play as "Our Town" but I guess I have to go along with the majority. Today for lunch I had a salmon salad sandwhich it was the first salmon salad that I've had in over a year and boy was it delicious. I finished the book on "The Art of Thinking" it was a very good and informative book. I am now reading some Thurber which is very funny and a book on Mythology. I think the mythology book is going to be one of the most influential books that I have ever read, I just have a feeling about it. It is an excellent book and it goes through various religions and the symbols and tales that each religion has adhereded to over the years. It also analyses what these various tales mean.

I have to leave the letter now and I'll mail it so that it comes to you tomorrow and I'll probably call you up tomorrow (thursday) afternoon.

Lots of Love

your son Robert

P.S. I just received a very nice letter from Jay. He is still receiving nice rejection notes on his short stories but he is writing and teaching and painting and very homesick, but I'm sure that he wrote to you too.

Friday March 15 1963

Dear Dad,

It was really good to see you yesterday. I'll be back to see you on Sunday when I hope you will be feeling even better than you did yesterday. I really admire your friskyness and good humor. My humor is picking up gradually. It seems that that is the way that all things must be done—gradually. I am really coming along in therapy now. The family conferences have really helped and I am beginning to see things that previously I just couldn't see. The weather here is delightful, still a little on the cold side but already things are starting to become green again. That reminds me I may start working with the gardener which should be fun. He gave me a plant the other day and I have it on my window sill. It is a strange looking plant but quite pretty. This morning after my doctors appointment I went down to Creative therapy to paint a picture. I have been painting picture portraits for the last few days and I decided to paint a picture of you from my memory. Well the picture did not look as handsome or as exact as I wanted it to. But the lady in charge—Mrs. Gollob said "it looks just like you robert is it a self portrait." So you can see that it looked something like you because I look something like you and if she thought that it looked like me—well it sounds rather involved no? Anyway it has a slight resemblance to you. Perhaps you can see it and my other paintings soon. I'll ask if I can bring them home one weekend when I get a weekend and you are home.

I often think of you dear dad. Your sence of humor, of your warmness and feeling for people, of your quickness of wit and the incisive way that you have with ideas. I think of your gentleness and the love that you have for your entire family. Even with all the fighting that I put up I want you to know that both mother and you are among the best parents that a child could ever ask for. Numerous times when I have needed you you have always been ready to help even at times that it was very difficult for you practically. When I look around me and see children who grew up without knowing what the term love meant I consider myself more than lucky to have two parents who care a great deal as to my stability and good health.

I have to close now because I have to go to an activity (I am still framing pictures this time I am framing one of the pictures that mother and I bought in woodstock a few years ago). Here's hoping that I find you on Sunday as well as you have been doing for the past few days.

Shalom and love
Your son Robert

Dear Mom and Dad,

Once again i think i am coming back to the world of reality. It is still frightening for me but less and less. I am going to most of my activities. I am really looking forward to seeing you on either the weekend or at the family conference that we planned.

Most of all I am beginning to understand that getting sick is no ones fault, that it just happens and we then have to go about getting well. I am also listening more to people now and trying to understand what they say. It is more difficult to understand what people are saying than what you or rather i hear.

I received mail from Aunt Esther Madeline and Jay and they were all very encouraging.

I'd like from now on for me to be honest for me to tell you the little things that annoy me when i'm with you. But these things are hard for me to do. I am frightened that you will punish me in some way or another. I know that you won't but I am still afraid that you will.

I am back to working on the newspaper again and it is fun. Friday a poet is going to come and read us some of his poems. I hope that he is a good poet. Monday night our unit is going to have a talent show and I volunteered to read some of my poems. I really should be writing this letter in longhand but I'm afraid that my handwriting is not that good or legeble.

with some of my love
robert

My first novel, Big Man, *was published in June, 1966. At the time, I was living at 150 West 76th Street, in New York City, and Robert—out of the hospital for nearly a year (he stayed at Hillside for eighteen months)—was living next door, with a friend he had made at Hillside, at 152 West 76th Street. On July 7, 1966, his house to mine, he sent me a Special Delivery letter, written partly in the style of* Big Man's *narrator.*

July 6, '66 7:AM

Jay

I'm about half way thru the Big Man it's been one of the important readings in my life—which has been filled with words. At first of course I started searching thru the books for references of me—after all if I'm going to be immortalized in one of the truer tales of the twentieth century the fucken author better get it right...well I found some resemblance and a whole lot of other familiar ammalgamations and alternated between fury, worse tears which was broken by just laffs for those of the prehistoric era—they're there alright but so is Mack, and Willa they live louder than those murmerings of jealousy.

Big Man may not be the Great American Novel but then Joel Campus [*my first novel, never published*] wrote that and who needs him and his ilk. And that is not excusing it to say that it passes, it scores I don't have to be the last one to tell you that you write. You write, when youre not listening to what should be said but what is said you do with words and characters what I would like to do with pictures I guess. But enough blurb.

I'm glad I didn't get to see this novel before. Until little ago I wasn't really ready for any new or novel. Somehow at this time in this place this day and some after the anniversary of what was once an american holiday I managed to start reading something by my big brother. Feeling free i now disown you of that titlte you're no longer my big brother. Jay Neugeboren will do.

There are things to be said but they will be or won't. There are going to be plenty of monday morning foul shooters so why bother. You somehow got it down, and its there bound for who knows whom or what gee—excelsior.

Me—there's no shit on me I got the dirtiest hands this side of Queens but those bitten down fingers are going to pound out something or other—brother through all the hallways and wanderings I'd try defaithing you'd like plastic man manage to stretch. If there ever appears on the american scene something by robert gary you know if nobody else cares to who his big man is. I want to return and then go on to the world which is scheduled for this wednesday i just had to take a break from one of the most exciting and angering morning watches i have been priveleged to make in this so short and (un) happy life i live.

I'm glad you're working on that other book already maybe I'll be able to read that one too soon.

love and some other four letter words
Robert

In the summer of 1966, shortly after the publication of Big Man, *at a time when I was driving across country to spend a year as Visiting Writer at Stanford University, Robert began having serious difficulties. In the fall of 1966, our parents tried to get him re-admitted to Hillside Hospital, but Hillside would not take him back, and so Robert began what was the first of at least three separate, long-term hospitalizations (to a total of about four and a half years) at Creedmoor Hospital, a New York state facility in Queens. He spent the majority of these years on Doctor Peter Laqueur's insulin coma ward.*

In the Spring of 1967, I left Stanford, drove east, crossed the ocean, and spent most of the next eighteen months with my wife Betsey in a small village (Spéracèdes) in the south of France. While we were living there my second novel, Listen Ruben Fontanez, *was published, and my wife, in the summer of 1968, suffered what seemed a miscarriage (the local French doctor thought it a false pregnancy).*

[*July 8, 1968*]

> to think of the two of you there
> in some De Gaulle town
> making funny noises when you should be here
> --but the war is almost over
> and let's hope there won't be another one
> spring slid into summer
> the hospitals hardly know me anymore
> and although there's no young damsel
> for me to undistress
> it seems that I'm almost out of my sweet mess
> it won't be long now
> before—before what?
> who's kidding whom
> I've already past a quarter century
> in this the worst of all possible worlds
> o well two more quarters left
> and then the game might be over yet.

*****

thought I'd send this cheerful little poem along to you and break my long but necessary silence. Things really are finally straightening out seeing that I don't really want to be any other place home is not that bad, the folks really do love me and I take all their advice with lots of salt.

I'm sorry Betsey dear that you had to lose the child, but I hope you are not feeling too badly about it. I am still looking forward to becoming an uncle in near or not too distant future.

Jay I read Hear Hear Rubin Fontanez. For a slow reader I found it very fast reading. I liked best the old man and part with the voo doo dolls. I thought the part of the dancing in the trains could have been developed and perhaps the frustration of teaching in the city schools. But then I didn't write the book. Congratulations on the offers from Penguin and Farrar. Mother still talks endlessly about her visit [to you] and I sometimes look at the bearded pictures that arrived.

I have finally a somewhat o.k. job. I don't know if mother told you but I was working in a specimen laboratory and I'd come home nauseous every evening. My first day out looking for another job I landed one with a film company. They do film strips and I make copies of the strips. It's a very easy job and I spend most of the time in the dark picking my nose but I'm going to see about becoming a camera man. You write that you hope the summer is bearable it is. I think that one needs a calendar to tell what season it is in New York. I finally saw what one can call a beautiful movie "Elvira Madigan"—it was photographed in a sort of faded color and fantastic photography MACK [*our cat, left with our parents in Queens*] JUST SHAT UP THE BATHTUB it was just a love story with a double suicide at the end and although it was very slow moving and the most silent of movies that I have seen in years it was very well done.

election day, nov. 5, 1984 [*1968*]

Dear Jay and Betsey,

Well that time is here again, the great democratic choice between twidledee and twidledum on the one hand tricky dick and on the other the great bore Hump and then if youre really batty edgar Wallace. Well I fooled them all I voted for the peace and freedom candidate Dick Gregory. Mother says I wasted my vote but I don't think so in this neighborhood Humphrey is sure to take a huge majority so I feel that I would have wasted my vote by going along with the farce. Of cource I'll be rooting for Hubert tonight when we watch the election returns and it would be a shame if the country this great an wonderful country of mine which sees fit to wage war for some rich vietnamese but refuses to fight for her own Negroes and that forgotten race the American Indian who was robbed of his land and rights. [*in margin, hand written:* "chooses Nixon (pissing, I lost the sentence—quick call up Faulkner)"] So when I entered the gymnasium of the defunct school and saw the Peace and Freedom party was on the ballot and I didn't have to vote for the communist candidate or write in my own name, I decided to vote for the funny man and Mark Lane.

The results should be in soon and I doubt if that rag of public journalism which I don't even bother to read any more except some sundays for the book lists and stamps advertising The New York Times will even print how many votes Dick Gregory got or any of the other minor candidates but there it is I want Peace and Freedom now not in 2084.

I was really excited to read about your writing a screenplay that really sounds exciting as the screen is I think the best 20th century medium for the exchange of ideas. I saw two great movies "The Heart is a Lonely Hunter" a screening of Carson McCullers book and last night on the TeeVee Fred (notice I can be familiar too!) Fellini's highly misunderstood "La Dolce Vita." The first had the same quality as one of my favorite movies "The Long Hot Summer" and I kept thanking the Lord or whoever one thanks that I can speak and hear. Also that I can see, I sure would hate to have to live in a dark world. La Dolce showed that life really isn't so sweet although Marcello sure had his share of Women.

Speaking of women I just spoke with Martha Schwartz nee Levy her daughter is talking already and she sounds fine although a bit lonely they are living out on the island somewhere in the Hamptons and she seems to be enjoying the country.

[*hand-written, bottom of page*] Look at all this space save it for a sunny day

February 5, 1969

Dear J&B

sorry to have received your last letter. From previous letters it seems you were quite close with Nancy [*a friend, in Spéracèdes, who committed suicide*] and the loss to you both must be great. I really don't know what to say or rather write. I do hope that this letter finds you in better spirits.

Nothing much is new here except that after giving my boss two weeks notice because I am taking a job with the post office I got fired for some silly excuse. It would have only meant working for two more days this week but I guess he found someone else. I didn't really enjoy getting fired but then I didn't really enjoy the job. Although I did enjoy all the reading I did on it, the last two books I read there were long ones Moby Dick and Jude the Obscure i enjoyed them both. If I ever write anything besides these silly poems I putter with, I would like it to be on the style of both. The all encapsulation of Moby (which I just now saw on T.V.—do you miss the boob tube?) and the dark tragedy of Hardy. They are really or rather were excellent writers. I did write a poem on Moby and may enclose it [*he did*] after looking it over I think it good enough. I did an awful lot of reading on the job. It was the simplest job I ever had. I think I explained it to you all I did was be a sort of baby sitter for a Rube Goldberg type machine. It got so that I would load it up and then run next door to read. I took the job with the Post Office because of the money and also returning to school. I'll be able to go full time finally, in the fall and just work summers. I'm sure the work won't be too interesting but then work usually isn't. Perhaps someday I'll be in the position you're in and be free of bosses and busy work. As mentioned I'm going back to school. I said to hell with the nightmares I've been having—one of which is a real wopper—it is usually in black and white the term is halfway over and I'm still looking for my math class. I'm taking Music, an English survey cource and they made me take gym. Well maybe I'll take off some of the weight I've been putting on sitting and sleeping. I lost about two pounds today because I took a haircut. I was thinking of sending you some of my locks but I hear you have plenty of hair of your own. I hope you keep your beard till you hit stateside as I'd like to see my brother as a somewhat beatnik—I think that we are in the beatnik generation not hippie. I did read your article from autobiography in NAR and thought it the best thing you have written so far (published that is). It had a clear maturity about it and I felt that I was reading from the writings of a great man. Your writing of Speracedes and the unity of your life made me envious. But then I have oft times been envious of the easy life.

We were almost on Television on the David Susskind show. It seems that Dr. Cott is going to be on and he wanted me as an example of the fine work he is doing with schizophrenics and their cure. I half toyed with the idea and then thought better of it not wanting to make a public spectacle of my delusions and not wanting to be deluded into thinking that the publicity surrounding the show would be about anything but my previous sickness(es). I did ask him if he thought therefore that I was cured. He said not exactly cured but at least arrested, and that if after five years i stayed about the same on the vitamins and with a reduction in them over that time and then afterwards he saw no reason why that term could not be applied.

The pills are working fine [*Dr. Cott believed in orthomolecular therapy: the administration of megadoses of vitamins*] and much more fun than making up stories for doctors and pseudodoctors. I am repulsed by all the talking that I once did and really don't know what I talked about and how those "professionals" could sit there and listen. But then I guess when youre getting paid at the rates that they are you can sit. I only have to see the good doctor once every two months and then only for a half hour and then I just about have enough to say to him. But he does have nice pictures in his office (among them original Klees, Picassos and Braques). By the way I don't think I ever thanked you for the Hiddieoyss Botsch you sent me it was really very nice and is hanging in the apartment. I'm going to get it this weekend as calling steve this week he gave me the good news that he is getting married in march. Of cource I wished him the best but god only knows what I am going to do with all the junk left in the apartment. Did you ever hear about the apartment that I took on top of him. I turned it into a studio for about a month and then meeting an old jazz friend took pity on him and took him in. The pity should have been for me however for he was a quite serious student of heroin. Well about that time I went into the hospital again for one of my readjustments (should I say annual) and when I came back found out that the damn fool had left the water running somewhere and flooded three apartments. So I took a loss and quickly hid my tail and came home. It isn't so bad living here. The folks are fine and as nice as can be expected although I make sure not to spend too much time home when they are here taking evening jobs. They are fine by the way and I'm sure you'll soon get a missile from mother with two lines attached from dad.

I think mom wrote that we had what could be called a new years party. It was bearable and I met a very nice girl whom I've been dating. Yes I'm actually dating a girl. There is nothing strange about her sorry to say. Her name is Eva and she does substitute teaching in a local high school while she is getting her masters in Spanish. She had exams and papers so I couldn't see her right away but we did speak to each other on the phone and then we went out a couple of times. The romance (not really a romance for though we 'like' each other we are not really in love) is cooling and although I saw her last night (we went to a concert at Carnegie Hall, the Cleveland orchestra playing prokoffiev and Bramms) she doesn't want to make it anything steady and so we will take a weeks leave. Saw a broadway show Saterday night. A modern rendition of Canterbury Tales which was mildly bawdy it had a rock beat but the rhyming of every two lines was almost inane. I'd like to get the music when it comes out in record form. I find myself limited to record buying because of not having a stereo...She's a very nice girl etc. etc and she even laffs at all my jokes she's not exceptionally pretty but she does have a beautiful moustache—o well I guess there will be enough girls to choose from at school and maybe at the post office. That was one of the reasons why I didn't like the job with Manhattan Color except for about an hour when I first came in I was all alone which gets boring. Thanks for the stamps by the buy but except for "La Dance" I had them already and paid about 35 cents for each did you pay more? There are some things I'd like you to get me if it's not too much trouble. A genuine french beret (blue preferably) and a small pipe of algerian briar. But then the french may not be importing algerian briar so if it's too much trouble forget about it.

Of the movies I've seen recently only one was any good "Candy" it was stupid but very funny and obsene. In movies these days it seems anything goes,. Also saw "2001" which was terribly boring. The fact that Big Man may be accepted was great news. It should make a very nice movie. What about the other movie you were working on never heard anything further on it. How are your books doing in England by the way...About my painting career I called it quits the produce was terrible.

ps Betsey I'm also reading Dickens, Great Expectations it's a pip of a book.

Love

XOX

Robert

Hey you'll be home soon. welcome home
(signed) Richard Nixon

2nd Shabbos Bermuda [*August, 1970*]

Cher tout,

haven't written because most was the usual. I mean I could have written that I was doing well improving feeling fit etc you know the old Hillside Jewish Child Care Bit but what the Heck.

Spent my first week a forsooken tourist getting in motorcycle accidents and buying fancy trinkets I've always wanted. Wound up at some peoples home and when I paid the rest realized I had about $20 for another week . She (the luv) suggested I phone up home — forgotten what awaited me

well after the pleasant preliminaries I SAID I guess you know why I called

-"why?"

money

come home

do you want me to eat

will send it

then mother wanted to tell me something for 10 minutes well that was not the end — instead of sending the money thru the banks (I would have received it thursday this was wed. nite) they wanted to mail it.

all right (But I still haven't goten it won't till Mon Tues or Wed. I go home Tues nite.) The drama is not over next thing the police arrive I'm to call home. They wanted me home I sounded "high" and they were worried they phoned Dr. Cott he "said" I should come home increase my medicine. I said if anything I would be called depressed. "Depressed?" come home we're worried. well. Dr. Cott called Friday morn we had a nice chat said he would speak with Mom quiet her down that I should increase (so I told him what pills I had taken more of) he said I probably was more shaken up by the motorcycle accidents than I conveyed to them, also that I was a fool to have fallen into the old tourist trap. He suggested I be a plutocrat and take taxis I [answered] back very easy for you to say. Dr's always seem to think that if you can afford them you can afford life.

Anyhow and way I have been on vacation feeling alternately like thoreau or allen ginsburg or really my old self in California.

The accidents were fun but more frightening. 4 of them. The doctor in the hospital SAID nothing was broken but did give me some darvan (which did next to nothing, I've finished off 2 bottles of aspirin and excedrin since and my arm still bothers me, thought I would play some tennis but doubt it now)

I'm sorry you were so disappointed in Jan's and mine little altercation but really although she can be a great mixer not only wouldn't she put out but she was more neurotic than some other mother we know. Well anyway wait until you meet Angie Cain—a shiksa of the first order.

well enough scribbling write me about the parents you've become [*our first child, Miriam, was born on January 2, 1970]*--time for an afternoon swim. I hope all the news at your end is equally as uninteresting—send my mere my love and tell her I meant to send some sort of souvenir but alas I come first.

Je t'aime

Frere Robert

P.S. I found the yellowing edition of Listen Ruben in the Bermuda Public Library. Nothing in the Book shops however.

That's good news!

You're an international author n'est ce pas

Luv Luv Luv

Robert

In the late spring of 1972, after being arrested, Robert was taken to the Mid-Hudson Psychiatric Center, a (forensic) hospital for the criminally insane. He wrote to me often from Mid-Hudson—long hand-written letters on the lined official stationery of the institution. His frustration became increasingly overt. "I wonder how many more years I shall have to spend in these Young Age Homes," he wrote in one letter. In another: "Please send to Dr. Tonkin a permission slip so that I can come visit you for the Pesach holydays—it would do so much for me and I guess the whole family for us to once again be together and on my birthday yet." Miriam was now two and a half years old; Robert's first letter from his new home was addressed to her.

Tuesday [*June, 1972*]

Dear Miriam

I bet you're bragging to all the other kids on that block of yours about your big time criminal of an uncle.

Well I regret and I now declare that I shall never again (if there was a first) assault and battery (what a charge—I made a pun I made a pun!) even a police official.

Maybe you could put together a package of magazines and paperbacks? I think I could start reading again—also maybe Betsey could find an old sketchbook

I thank you for your beautiful letter I still sometimes read it

But it was only one

Also thanx for the sour balls But the ward got hold of them however and they lasted one afternoon

nothing to write all is boorsville

please write soon as I miss you.

o yeah the folks were here momma was so scared they stayed 45 minutes

love
Robert Neugeboren #247

Jayson

Many happy returns on another birthday—I put away an inter-
changable present but it needs a little more money $ maybe for
your next birthday

Mid-Hudson Valley Hospital
June 12 (XII) 1972 AC

Dear Nieces and Nephews

It has been many moons since I nervously presided as something called Best Man at the conuptual connniptions of your loving parents. Now look at them they cant even cook a meal without each anothers help let alone lead someone out the front lawn (your wedding lawn) without eagerly tearing into them as if they were a juicy piece of (d)uck. Miriam—when they tell those others the illiterati to go climb a tree do they hand the guest a xeroxed map. Any which way—Bonne Happy Anniversaire and Betsey the next time you [drink] the John Daniels have one for me.

For your wedding anniversary give him (or her) these beautifully sensitive deeply moving LOVE POEMS OF MARRIAGE, by Evelyn Barkins author of the bestseller, "The Doctor Has a Baby" and other outstanding books—this little gem of a volume will inscribe your love indelibly on your mates heart—and will be treasured forever—from an ad in NY times—also get this line from a review of a book *Ringalevio*

It was a grand enterprise supported by Grogan's canny and sweat. It is in this area that he is most interesting...

How blew are you?

Do you think I should send it in to the New Yorker? I also read that Albert Camus is finally celebrating a *Happy Death*—mazel tov—is it true that some more Neugeborens are getting married? One mazel tov per letter is enuf. But if you show your faces or feces at the weddings (I warn you cousin Gerald will be there and he may bring his tephillan) and they ask after me (you know Jay didn't you once have a brother and there was something wrong with him there was even a book about him painting his pictures out of an institution) tell them I smoke cigars and really do love them and that with my next face lift I'll look better than never.

I'm gonna be a 2nd uncle. That sounds terible. I am an uncle and once an uncle always an uncle only knights used socks.

Dr. Ken Blatt [*a friend*] comes here and guppahs. The "folks"come and moon. And soon too soon I meet with Jessica again.

For a writer you sure don't write much but thanks anyway for the remittance but you didn't have to make the check out to A.D.A. I mean Hubert is defunct. I did some sketches, but it seems I am always doing sketches this whole letter has been a sketch. Anyway they were in colour (yes miriam I am a liberal and some of my best friends...and am proud of them. My parents—I guess they are yours too you want to choose?) sent a care package also my art teacher Jules Mervin sent one which was being held up downstairs while I am being held up upstairs. I read constantly and offer this verse in closing.

you people, rather my brothers family has trees
the way some dogs have fleas

> Brother Bagel
> Midst Hudson's Unit
> Je m'appelle Robt Neugeboren
> 28th de Juin

Greetings to each and everyone of you (and this aint Uncle Sam) When you guys said you were putting down roots I didn't think you meant you would allow the good earth to engulf you. How come no lettuce? not the season? Anyway I'm towards my way out and will not have to go back to court just a short stay at a state hospital (probably more of a creed since it is close to the folks and I no longer have an address) (But I did get a hat)

Am reading and rereading … (*Demian* and *Huck* with all his "love and death") other books I devour and am also sketching and even writing again. Here is one I composed in the stillness of last night

> The Winbreakers
> Daily devotional disciplines
>   no apologee to Gerard Manny
> He caught this morning mornings minyan
>   making daylight
> His kingdom of Judea (taking) naps at dawn
> (yawn). outside. Falcons fast flying by
> the Rabbi steadily striding sliding schul wards

"Hi there" how had he brung together those wedding
                                                              birds
Some extasy or something boy could he swing
Silky smooth as the roller skates he used to glide with
Now he even rebuffed their breaking wind
                 (the culprits hiding)
Stirring an egg the Rebitzen at home was
                                   waiting
Truth, duty firmness and oh air soon the
                              seventeen prayers
His buckle! and oh the fire that broke from her
        then—6 million also put to fire and
        worser – 'ahav-ha-shalom'. but my chevalier
        No danger now--still lovely
No wondrous thing; pine plodding schtups this
        plough neath the dark down
Shine on harvest moon
Sad a lovely tune
I hope the Jesuits don't come after me not too long now and I'll
be sitting neath the shade of all your cherry trees Tell Miriam that
Uncle Robert often considers her in his prayers and thoughts and
hopes she is not growing up too fast. The folks write that she is "a
regular young lady"—well I should hope so we have enough irreg-
ulars in the family—me myself I guess an an irregular 36 but not a
lady.
        need I say more
        soon you'll be four
        alright willa [*our dog*] five (not to mention your revolving cat
plan!)
                              love
                              RBG and Bklyn Bobby

Mid-Hudson Psychiatric Center
[July, 1972?]

Hi, Hi Hi

No news here i either sleep or read also eat and take my lithium like a good boy. I'm told I look good so there must be a bar mitzvah soon. The folks came by shabbos with the chicken and all the news about who's dying and who isn't

I sure am glad you have a gallery Betsey. Does that mean that you are painting again. That would be good news. Jules Mervin sent some paints and now some art books—he confessed in one of his letters that he doesn't even have a B. A.

I put myself in charge of a newspaper here but can't get anyone to write for it plus don't know what to write about. This place is so vacant. I hope my niece Miriam Nancy enjoyed the New Year and her grandparents—they are so proud of her—I am too and miss her—(send more of her drawings)

I don't seem to be moving from here very soon and they are going to move to a new place called New Hampton—but by the time we get there it'll be more like olde Hampton.

I wrote away for some info on that 'special' school near you 'Hampshire College.' but for $4300 they don't seem to offer much except for chairless lounges.

Have been reading again *Zorba* which I think was overrated, *The Point of No Return* by the late John P. Marquand whom I think was one of your favorites Jay, it was really an excellent book in the old style of a novel. Dad brought up some of my paperbacks and am currentoly reading Justine by Durrell. Boy can he write, sensuous too. My only regret is that I have to wait to read the rest of the tetrology.

There is some hope that I can get a pass and Ken Blatt will probably take me somewhere in the neighborhood. I guess Hyde Park is too long a trip but if we get there you think I'll get special attention? please write, type and send pictures as every day I wait for mail like some P.O.W.

Listen one favor—I would like to correspond again with Ben Saltman my old friend and teacher at Emerson [experimental college in California that Robert attended]. In the edition of "Works" that your short story was in (Elijah?) there was an ad from some out of the way publisher for a small book of poetry of his. Maybe they would forward a letter from me. Thanks.

Keep well don't work too hard and forget about the publishers — let 'em publish crap

Your languishing frere
Robert Gary

Mid-Hudson Psychiatric Center
[Fall, 1972]

May the blessings of the ancient una chaplin sana token be upon your house and barn and may all your trees seek their own aleyas. So whom is or was Gloria Ginsberg? I don't believe she was a fink was I supposed to marry her and ran away to Gracie Square instead. I hope her children are fine she sounds balabatush.

Jacob that was really your best letter in many moons (thats about how often I get them) I mean not only does your return to the faith seem less or more than comical but your attitude to the American Book Business (we all know that they are run by Jews Communists and Finks so you shouldn't do too bad) seems healthy — it is good to be healthy mon frere — take it from one of the favorite subsidized patients of all forms of insurance in New York State (I am applying for Social Security and bet I retire before the folks!)

Any way you write I should phone anytime etc very good but one thing dont forget — a telephone number. You know in this country we use digit dialing. I guess all I have to do is call up Massachusetts and ask for the Neugeborens who doesn't know the Neugeborens you know etc etc. So please send a phone number and the best time to call as I'm liable to get only Samela [*cat*] at home and we don't even know each other.

Forgot to mention 3 other books I read — *The Genius & the Goddess* by A. Huxley it was really engrossing rapid reading and specio philosophical *The Greening of America* what a turkey! this guy Charles A. Reich quotes Marcuse Marx and some others but the whole affaire is like a Readers Digest reworking of a Sunday times special supplement on don't worry folks your children are justified in wearing long hair. How he comes up with the ecological Greening business I'll never know the whole tract is political and sociological. Somehow I managed to read it as if it was my duty to get an education. (Remember—R. Gary Neugeboren observor of the American Scene?) also finished James Baldwins "Blues for Mister Charlie" which also was disappointing in that it was mostly cliches. Don't forget Ben Saltzman or some paperbacks or 'little' magazines but most of all don't forget your heritage boy. And I forgot don't forget those pads which had DON'T FORGET in red on top—ever remember anything you ever wrote on them?

Love again
Robert Gary

Mid-Hudson Psychiatric Center
[*1973*]

Dearest Miriam

Tell your parents that I am jealous first one has a showing then the other goes and publishes another book by holt Rinehart and Winston (a brand I never smoke).

and tell your daddy that I appreciate all the books he sent but do I have to read all of them?

listen nothing good new here yet hope the baby is on its way

love

Robert Gary (frere)

found a new pen almost time for chow wanted to tell you how much how very much I miss your parents and you even now

love again

frere and oncle Robert

Robert was transferred from Mid-Hudson to Creedmoor during the summer of 1973. In mid-October when our parents left Queens for West Palm Beach, Florida, where they had bought a two-bedroom apartment in Century Village, a retirement community, Robert was still at Creedmoor. Our father, who died of emphysema three years later, never saw Robert again. Our mother, who died on July 12, 2003 (she had Alzheimer's disease since 1992 and had been living in a nursing home in Florida), had, from 1973 to 2003, seen Robert twice.

Thursday Nov 15 1973

Dear Jay and family (yes you too Betsey Betsey even my niece and nephew [*Aaron, born January 12, 1973*] but especially Willa [*dog*] Mack [*cat*]

Well all's going well if slowly here nothing to complain about yet nothing much to report. I am still at the hospital and it seems for never till I'll get into Boerum Hill-Hall but I'm sure the wait will be worth it. I come to school everyday do some math problems eat my sandwich lunch do some more and then at 2:30 head home. I generally walk from the subway to the Hospital both to save the carfare and for the walk. School is alright I'm up to Algebra and soon I'll start drafting, which is what I'm really looking forward to.

Speaking of looking forward, I thought perhaps that I could spend Thanksgiving weekend with you but the Doc says that I would not be allowed to cross state lines by myself which would mean you (Jay) would have to come pick me up and bring me home that would be too much so I am spending thanksgiving day with Rita and her family. She is an older girl (or woman) who has already been married and has 3 children but we get along very well together—she has a nice disposition and sence of humor as well as good looking—she is very much in luv with me! You know I miss the folks but they seem to be doing fine so all power to them in their move.

Its Tuesday now the class is almost over and I'll be taking the trip back out to the funny farm. Have to return 2 books (Gurdieff's *Meetings with Remarkable Men* and Robert Nathan's *Mind*) both of which I happened to actually read. Yes, I can read now and I really enjoy racing through books am currently reading *The Way of All Flesh* by Samuel Butler and Amerika by Franz Kafka. Both of which are excellent accounts of different times, different life styles.

So the latest is Thanksgiving w the Perlas [cousins] Carolyn Louis and family and aunt Ethel and Uncle Nat Cohen. But I did spend Saturday with Rita we went to a free show at Hunter a musical about the West. It had its charm and the authoress and old Geezer was sitting in the row ahead of us. Sunday I walked 5 miles each way to see the Streisand Redfeld move at the Parsons—very sweet but the politics were a jumble—just when you think Hollywood could say something sensible.

Well I hope the green is still green and all the trees are well as well as the swimming and I guess sooner or later we'll get to see and be with each other. I must say that I really enjoyed our short visit that moving Sunday.

Miss you all very much.

Now me go eat Chinese

Love Love love
brother Robert

May 3, 1973

Dear Jay and Betsey and Miriam and Aaron and Willa and
Samela

Well I am breaking down and writing you guys a letter. This
typewriter has been here for some time only I didn't know about it
now that I know I'll catch up on all my correspondance.

You have no idea how great I felt at your place. Your hospital-
ity was over perfect. (Just spoke to the folks, nice dry conversation
with how are you's galore) I'm going to interrupt this letter to clean
up this room a chore assigned me. The place is shining not yet spot-
less but shining. Please tell me what to do with my feet. They are
still bothering me like crazy I am writing this letter with my left leg
pinned underneath my seat it seems to calm me that position. But i
still can't watch any television.

How are your trees. It was so nice to see your arboretum but
not all the work that goes into keeping it up—you seemed to know
what you were doing in between arguments to the contrary.

At the rate I'm going niece Miriam will be able to visit me at a
half-way house something they definitely have from Midhudson
State also lots of rehabilitative services so I'm told. (I better slow
down on this old machine i'm not as good typist as I thought. You
know what I love—Jay's typewriter especially the numbers on it. I
like it better when you write.

So now that you've finished the screenplay and your novel
what are you going to attempt next Jayson? I hope something good.
Me I'm going to end this funny or funky letter and wish you the
best of luck and the healthiest of springs nice talking to you betsey.

loads of love
Robert

[Creedmoor]
Feb 14, 1974
St. Valentines Day

Dear Jay

Thanks for a copy of your new book [*Sam's Legacy*]. Have been waiting for mail for so long from either you or the folks and now this big black book arrives. It looks terrific and you should feel proud. I shall try and start reading it tonight.

I hope the folks are alright I haven't gotten any mail from them in over a month—then I haven't written to them either but they do usually write. I was very worried but I guess all is well with them.

My girlfriend went down to Florida with her children for two weeks and I miss her—she won't be back until Sunday.

School is alright—I do the work but I still do messy drawings.

It seems I shall be here at Creedmoor for an awfully long time as there has been a holdup and delay in Welfare on account of the transfer from NYCity to Federal funding with me caught in the middle. I don't think Boerum Hill would be that much better but I would like to get out of here and away from these sick people. It has been agreed in Dr. Hyde's absence (illness & vacation) that I can get a part-time job—weekends and one or 2 evenings a week. Jobs are very scarce especially part-time ones.

I realize that Aarons birthday past with no recognition from his ailing uncle. I'll try to send something belated anyway but really have no idea other than another "toy."

Also it was Miriams birthday again (already!) well Obert presents just aint what he used to be I might as well tell you how oncle obert absconded with some funds. I receive $10 a week from O.V.R. through Mrs. Mortimer for carfare and small extras. Well in the meantime these 3 checks $20 each come addressed to me so I immediately visited my friends at the bank. Well of course Mrs. Mortimer found out and now it was decided that I pay back $1 a week and if I get a job more.

I still read a lot nothing great some Science Fiction (trying to read something by my old friend Sam Delaney but it is difficult) did read *Nine Stories* again and thought them excellent. Also *Local*

Anesthetic by Gunter Grass, short stories by Isak Dienstein rather obscure, essays by Geo Orwell interesting but pedantic, a good Sci Fi by Simak which I stayed up all one night to finish and I don't remember what else. Glance at the papers they took out the tee Vee (but when at Ritas we watch) and I have taken up doing crossword puzzles almost insanely. I can sometimes even almost finish them.

I go to the movies often but haven't seen anything good since Jacques Tati's "Playtime"—fell asleep at the Godfather, was turned off by "Lady Sings the Blues" last weekend saw "The Getaway" which was alright in that they did get away and Ali Magraw is one of my favorites. With it was a john Huston western "Judge Roy Bean" it was much superior to the general Western and then saw "Deep Throat"—very sophomoric and not even that dirty though it attempted smuttiness.

"Sleeper" supposed to be in a class with Chaplin and Buster Keaton (although he reminds me of Harry Langdon more than the first two) Went to the Museam of Modern Art last Wednesday from school. Their admission is up to $1.75 but I could get in cheaper as a student I believe—I have something like a business card that says I go to Manhattan Technical Institute anyway their policy is pay what you want on Wednesdays so I donated $.18 and promptly went up to the members lounge and had a Manhattan also lost a good pipe there.

One Shabbos I went to the neighborhood temple for services—it was nice and I really enjoyed myself. I even got an "aliyah" and could manage to read along in the Torah. I don't remember ever really reading in a Torah and I was really impressed by the beauty and perfection of the script. I guess I'll go back. They have nice kiddushes too but a very small congregation.

Hope all is well where you are—I was glad that you could dedicate the book in part to the memory of Betsey's parents. I miss them and I'm sure Betsey does too—it was very unfortunate that they past away so young and missed the joy of seeing the grandchildren grow up and there children prosper.

I hope "a good time was had by all" in Century Village and I'm sure the parents were thrilled to have the both of you and their grandchildren there. I'm sure they both spoiled and showed off their little treasures.

I guess those other two are fine I mean

[*drawings of Mack the cat, and Willa the dog*]

How much do you weigh Mack? I'm up to 165 (Willa could sue me)

Well anyhow be good a hearty MAZEL TOV!

And please write

> Love
> XOX Uncle Robert
> [*with self portrait*]

Tell Miriam that I have a picture of her looking after Aaron and it rests on top of my bookcase and I can look at it constantly.

I went to mail this and I don't even have your home address – it has been so long since I've written so am sending it to you at school. But please send Betsey my best and fondest regards as I do miss all of you.

> love
> your brother

seeing their grandchildren growing up and their
children prosper.

I hope "a good time was had by all", in
Century Village, and I'm sure the parents were
thrilled to have the better of you and their
grandchildren Adam. I'm sure they both spoiled
and shoved off their little treasures.
I guess those other two are fine I mean

how much do you
weigh or make them
up to 185

(wish could see me)

Well anyhow be good & hearty
Mazel Tov!

Miriam

have have
one of her looking out Please write
again and the
keeper of my Love
— and I
us at it
my

* ☆ ❋ Uncle Bert

friday   may 24,1874

dear brother sister neice and nephew
glad to speak that i have come out of hibernation and feel
myselfagain.
hope all your green thumbs are dethorned.
i am very busy practicing my typing so tyat i may work for
the library and intend to start attemding something called
the Institue for the crippled and disabled.It will be a
a testing typ of programand i guess wham i fish i will
get a diploma stating that i am crippled and disabled.
also it will tell my ovr worker what sort of a school i shoul
aply for.Have looked for reviews of SAM'S LEGASY in the NY.Times
but have seen none I hope it does well.I thought it a top
—notheh novel with a very sympathetic rendering of all the
major characters.Hope it does well.
I have not much to write other than Rita is going through
with divorce proceedings and would like me to move in.
I don't see how i can take on such resposibility but
being that she is so good to me will continue seeing her.
not much more to write please keep in touchand I
hope Betsey is still painting will write soon and don't forget

HAPPY BIRTHDAY ONCE MORE
happy birthday

          love
              brother robert

friday may 24, 1874 [*1974*]

dear brother sister niece and nephew

glad to speak that i have come out of hibernation and feel myself again.

hope all your green thumbs are dethorned

I am very busy practicing my typing so that i may work for the library and intend to start attending something called the Institute for the crippled and disabled. It will be a testing type of program and i guess when i fish i will get a diploma stating that i am crippled and disabled. also it will tell my ovr [office of vocational rehabilitation] worker what sort of a school i should apply for. Have looked for reviews of SAM'S LEGACY in the NY Times but have seen none I hope it does well. I thought it a top-notch novel with a very sympathetic rendering of all the major characters. Hope it does well.

I have not much to write other than Rita is going through with divorce proceedings and would like me to move in. I don't see how i can take on such responsibility but being that she is so good to me will continue seeing her. not much more to write please deep in touch and I hope Betsey is still painting will write soon and don't forget

HAPPY BIRTHDAY ONCE MORE

happy birthday

love

brother robert

June 27, 1974

Dear jay and Betsey and all the little ones
Stop
Thanks for the New American Review I read almost the whole
thing before it was stolen and did like the "Ragtime" bit. Also liked
the biographical story on Henke's mother, and read the long article
on the flea not understanding very much about it.

Spent Monday with the Cohens and had a very nice time. Even
met Mark and his two sons. They go to a summer camp in i think
Springfield so Mark is thinking of calling you up when they go up
there to visit. Sarah and Marvin left for Russia today for a short
vacation. They said that when they come back they will take me out
again. They were really very kind to me and made me feel like one
of the family.

You asked where I type from. Well I am now in the typing class
(not for long as Monday I BECOME A CRIPPLED) (they'll finally decide that i am best suited to being a mentle patient) I come in
the mornings to practice and G-d only knows what I due in the
afternoons. Yesterday we had an indoor picnic due to the weather.
(Also Sunday Rita prepared a whole picnic lunch which we had to
consume indoors)

I am really feeling much better but at the present rate of
progress it seems like I'll be here forever. I spoke with a friend from
the post office and there is a possibility that if Boerum Hill doesn't
work out (although the social worker checked and I am still on the
waiting list) I could move in with him, I think we'd get along fine.
Although his apartment is all the way up in the Bronx.

As for Rita and I we see each other every weekend (now she
says that she would like me to come over during the week which I
may do sometime when I start this new program—which is only
for five weeks). We go to the movies sometimes even visiting. Her
two oldest children will be gone for the summer the girl to girl
scout camp and the boy to regular sleepaway which costs somewhere in the neighborhood of $1500 the youngest (almost Miriams
age 5 going on 6) is going to a day camp sponsored by the CYO
(Rita herself once converted to Catholicism sometime in her youth
for I don't know what reason). She is quite serious about me and

speaks of marriage and more children and i do not know how to answer her. Two saturdays ago I arrived early only to be greeted by Rachel (the older girl) saying my mother's not home BUT MY FATHER IS well we shook hands and came out fighting. Not saying anything to each other it was almost pleasant (you know they are not divorced yet only separated—yet he also has a girl friend where he lives) well when he left we shook hands again.

have to stop now
started the new program today and it looks good
See ya

love
Robert

[*Amchute Manufacturing Corporation letterhead*]
September 24, 1974

Dear Jay and Betsey and all the many little ones,

boy some delivery system, huh? [*our third child, Eli Chaim, was born on September 22, 1974*] I do hope that everything is going well and as expected. I bet Miriam is anxious though to see her new sybling.

Me I already bought a box of cigars (they are called "Longfellows") if that has any significance) and am handing them out even prematurely. Oh yes the letter head. That famous Institute that I attended came through and got me this job. It is mostly clerical work but that is to change. The secretary whose job I have took sick with some sort of brain damage and they had me filling in for her. Answering the phone, taking care of the mail, typing some letters and forms and some easy bookkeeping. But she seems better and is returning Monday. Well I thought I would have to revert to my crippled and disabled role but no. They like me so much here that I am going to do some detail work and also help around the office. Most of my work has been for Wingate Sales which sells Cross pens and also distributes pens to rehabilitation places such as IC. Amchute which is run by a Mr. Jason S. Siegel deals in all sorts of chutes. Mail, linen, trash and just general drops. So I'll be mostly working for them.

Still living at the house (Boerum) and if I can contine with this job and they decide to charge me room and board (which would be over $425 a month) I'll have to find some other arrangement. All so soon.

But I do feel good/find no major problems and am so glad to be back with the living.

Sat. I treated Rita to see "Over Here" which should have stayed there although the Andrews sisters were good and funny. Afterwards we went to a famous Swedish restaurant called the Stockholm—a smorgasbord affair and boy did we stuff ourselves. She started school this week—also clerical and is not too happy about it. She is toying with the idea of reconciliation with her husband but I think it is more his idea. If it should be over between the two (really five) of us that might be alright with me. But on the other hand or something she often asks when are we getting married, and talks about the folks as in-laws and is quite concerned that they are coming to visit soon and how she should host them. Also she would like more babies. Not me. (I think I should be more careful but that might just be my paranoia). Also Rita might go to Hungary for a little while and wants me to stay with the children. I don't think they should mind, and I guess they would be no trouble so I said I would stay with them—but I'm not sure if such a thing or arrangement would be right. It it were up to Rita (I call her Ritka) I could move in tomorrow but I know that would be wrong and detrimental.

Well harvest is here—I was wondering if you would be able to set up some sort of Sukkie (?) for Sukkoths and exactly what has ripened this year. I wonder what Miriam is like by now. Aaron I hardly know he was just a baby when I last saw him but Miriam Nancy must be a regular lady by now. I know she is quite busy and if she likes perhaps she could send some of her crayonned drawings I really dig them and would put up a good one or two in my room. I guess Betsey finds it hard to paint now but didn't you write that she was having another exhibit or show? I feel ready to paint again and was contemplating taking some sort of course. Would the two of you recommend The Brooklyn Museum Art School as I could commute there easily. Otherwise I was thinking of starting at the Art Student's League.

The folks sound sound and they seem much caught up in entertaining and getting together with their new found friends. Also so many of their old friends (even the Pauls) have moved close. Although I miss them I am very happy for them.

Saw a review by Jerry Charyn in the Times Book Review also at Abraham and Strauss your book (Sam) was either in the Best Seller of Times Recommend and there were only two copies left with room for maybe six. They were selling it for around $6.35—If you have by any chance any of my poems from the olden days I would appreciate if you would notify me. I can not seem to locate my friend whom I trusted with the nly last remaining copies of my major poems. I believe dad discarded everything but there might be something in the trunk. anyway don't spend too much time looking if you know of some just write as it would be reassuring. Also please write more often as I do get lonesome for some good news.

I know youre not having visitors but I (we) should like to see you and the new arrival so write soon rsvp as to your wishes. If youre not careful they'll take you out of the guide books.

anyway a happy a healthy new year and don't forget to repent love with some honey for the new year

brother robert

I had kippers today

Mid-Hudson Psychiatric Center
Monday aft
[*September 20, 1976*]

Dear Jay (and family)

Well here I am again and it's not a short story. The truth is "the" parents reneged on my visit and now aunt Mary (Weinberger—not SAPISSTEIN!) is now listed in the N. Y. Supreme Court as not only my codefendant but also: as "my mother," meanwhile I always thought I favored Uncle Arnold [*Mary's husband*] but at least I made it thru bailhood

Please write and tell my niece Miriam Nancy that I would appreciate some hard fruited candies!!!

Also tell her that I received her last letter when I was living in Manhattan on 25th Street. It was a very handsome note and I put it and the addressed envelope in my new safe deposit box at the Franklin Savings Society. I also bought (2) souvenir sheets (the appollo one) and I think if she (my niece) would like to trade some used (they're worth more than even the minted copies) from her UN collection I would be willing.

Ask Master Aaron (the talker) Bendorf if he would prefer ice skates or a new tennis racket to the baseball mitt I promised him?? (as I do not know his size!)

Maybe the whole troop including Eli Chaim and his mother could visit with me & you soon I would like to see my in-laws.

Jay please don't worry about me as I had "glandular (the kissing disease) fever" again and I think the "swine flu" and am coming out in fine shape.

If you do come or can't could you send some signs and a pipe and some good tobacco from either John's or in Amherst

Jacob I miss you very much please write or type a response
R.S.V.P.

Robert Schleeta
your kid brother
frere Robt Gary

P.S. I forgot to add that I loved your new book and so did Dr. Lewis (could you phone her—I also could receive calls

P.P.S. Jay and Betsey! Please subscribe me to the "N. Yorker" for Chanukah